For the Lord thy God. bringeth thee into a good land, a land of brooks of water, of fountains and depths that spring out of valleys and hills ; a land of wheat, and barley, and vines, and fig trees , and pomegranates; a land of olive oil and honey; Deut. 8 - 7 / 8

OUR VISIT TO ISRAEL

EMMANUEL DEHAN

A SPECIAL NEW EDITION IN COLOUR
REVISED, ENLARGED, UPDATED AND REILLUSTRATED

Other books by Emmanuel Dehan: Jacob's Well — Samaria*
Megiddo — Armageddon**
Come with me to Kinneret

*   French, German, Spanish and Italian
** French and German
Our Visit to Israel — French and German

Acknowledgement is here made for permission kindly granted for use and reproduction of photographs, illustrations and maps by the following:

Rolf Kneller, Jerusalem: Air view of Jerusalem — outside cover (front)

David Harris, Jerusalem: Plain of Gennesaret — outside cover (back)

Photo Garo, Jerusalem: Photographs

Carta, Jerusalem: Road maps of Israel

Amir's Publishers, Tel-Aviv: Details from maps of Jerusalem

Holyland Hotel, Jerusalem: Model of Jerusalem — partial views

Israel Museum, Jerusalem: King David, Rothschild Manuscript 24*
The Psalms Scroll (Dead Sea Scrolls)*
* Exhibits at the Israel Museum and the
Shrine of the Book — Jerusalem

Written, edited, designed, photographed and published by Emmanuel Dehan, P.O.B. 3238, Tel-Aviv, Israel.   Printed in Israel

Distributed in the U.S.A. by **Bloch Publishing Company**, 915 Broadway, New York, N.Y. 10010, Tel: (212) 673-7910

ISBN — 0-8197-0031-2.

And the Lord spake unto Moses, saying, Send thou men, that they may search the land of Canaan, which I give unto the children of Israel.. and Moses sent them to spy the land.. And they came unto the brook of Eshcol, and cut down from thence a branch with one cluster of grapes, and they bare it between two upon a staff.. And they told him, and said, We came unto the land.. and surely it floweth with milk and honey.

Numbers 13: 1, 17, 23, 27.

VISIT TO ISRAEL

A Visitor's Guidebook & Companion

CONTAINING A HISTORY AND GENERAL SURVEY OF ISRAEL, USEFUL INFORMATION, 260 COLOUR PICTURES — VIEWS, 17 MAPS AND DETAILED DESCRIPTION OF TOURING ROUTES THROUGHOUT THE COUNTRY, HISTORY AND BIBLE REFERENCES OF PLACES VISITED.

AN APOCRYPHAL PSALM

(PS. 151)

A Hallelujah of David the son of Jesse

1. *Smaller was I than my brothers and the youngest of the sons of my father,*
so he made me shepherd of his flock and ruler over his kids.

2. *My hands have made an instrument and my fingers a lyre;*
and (so) have I rendered glory to the Lord, thought I, within my soul.

3. *The mountains do not witness to him nor do the hills proclaim;*
the trees have cherished my words and the flocks my works.

4. *For who can proclaim and who can bespeak and who can count the deeds of the Lord? Everything has God seen, everything has he heard and he has heeded.*

5. *He sent his prophet to annoint me, Samuel to make me great; My brothers went out to meet him, handsome of figure and appearance.*

6. *Though they were tall of stature and handsome by their hair, the Lord God chose them not.*

7. *But he sent and took me from behind the flock and annointed me with holy oil;*
and He made me leader of his people and ruler over the sons of his covenant.

The Psalms Scroll from Cave II (The Elizabeth Hay Bechtel Psalms Scroll) one of the best preserved of the Dead Sea Scrolls. It contains 38 Psalms, arranged differently than the Massoretic order, in addition it included 7 Apocryphal Psalms, 3 of which were not previously known. (Exhibit at the Shrine of the book, Israel Museum, Jerusalem).

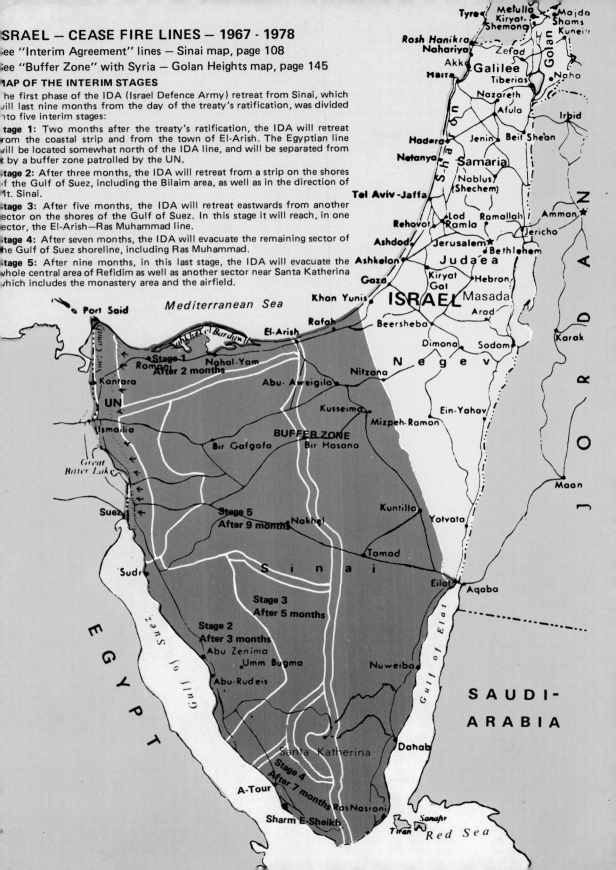

ISRAEL — CEASE FIRE LINES — 1967 - 1978

See "Interim Agreement" lines — Sinai map, page 108
See "Buffer Zone" with Syria — Golan Heights map, page 145

MAP OF THE INTERIM STAGES

The first phase of the IDA (Israel Defence Army) retreat from Sinai, which will last nine months from the day of the treaty's ratification, was divided into five interim stages:

Stage 1: Two months after the treaty's ratification, the IDA will retreat from the coastal strip and from the town of El-Arish. The Egyptian line will be located somewhat north of the IDA line, and will be separated from it by a buffer zone patrolled by the UN.

Stage 2: After three months, the IDA will retreat from a strip on the shores of the Gulf of Suez, including the Bilaim area, as well as in the direction of Mt. Sinai.

Stage 3: After five months, the IDA will retreat eastwards from another sector on the shores of the Gulf of Suez. In this stage it will reach, in one sector, the El-Arish—Ras Muhammad line.

Stage 4: After seven months, the IDA will evacuate the remaining sector of the Gulf of Suez shoreline, including Ras Muhammad.

Stage 5: After nine months, in this last stage, the IDA will evacuate the whole central area of Refidim as well as another sector near Santa Katerina which includes the monastery area and the airfield.

CHRONOLOGICAL TABLE

The Patriarchs: Abraham, Isaac and Jacob	1700—1400	B.C.
Exodus from Egypt	1350	
Arrival (and inheritance) in the Promised Land	1300—1250	
Judges: Deborah, Gideon	1200—1030	
Saul, first King in Israel	1030—1011	
King David	1011—	*
King Solomon, builder of the First Temple (950)	972—933	**
Division of the Kingdom: Judah and Israel	933	***
Samaria and Northern Kingdom destroyed	721	
Jerusalem and Temple destroyed by Babylon	587	
Return from exile in Babylon	537	
Building of Second Temple in Jerusalem	520	
Return to Zion under Ezra and Nehemiah	445	
Alexander the Great — Conquest	333	
Hellenistic rule	323—168	
Maccabees (Hasmonean) Revolt	167	
Beginning of Roman rule	63	
End of Hasmonean dynasty	37	
King Herod the Great	37—4	
Birth of Jesus	5	
Great Revolt of Jews against Romans	66—70	A.D.
Destruction of Jerusalem and Temple	70	
Fall of Masada — last stand against Romans	73	
Bar-Kochba's Revolt against Romans	132—135	
Revolt of Galileans against Romans	352	
Divison of Roman Empire — West & East (Byzantine) . .	395	
Byzantine rule	395—637	
Arab conquest	637	
Crusader conquest and rule	1099—1291	
Mameluke period	1291—1516	
Ottoman (Turkish) conquest and rule	1516—1917	
Return to Zion — beginning of settlement	1870	
Theodor Herzl — founder of Zionist movement	1895	
British Mandate — Balfour Declaration	1917	
State of Israel established (15 May)	1948	
(Israel's War of Independence)		
Sinai Campaign	1956	
Six Day War (5-10 June)	1967	
The "Yom Kippur" War (6 October)	1973	
"Interim Agreement" on Sinai signed (1 Sept.)	1975	
President Sadat's visit to Jerusalem (Nov. 19-20)	1977	
Prime Minister Begin's visit to Ismailia (Egypt) Dec. 25 .	1977	

*1011—961 (?), **961—922 (?), ***922 (?).

THE STATE OF ISRAEL, in the Near or Middle East, was established in 1948. It is in the continent of Asia, on the eastern seaboard of the Mediterranean, and is surrounded and bordered by four Arab countries: Lebanon in the north, Syria and Jordan in the east and Egypt in the south-west. Close to Africa (Egypt, across Sinai and the Suez Canal), and Europe (north, above Turkey), and small as it is, Israel, formerly part of Palestine, has been a battleground in its long history. Its geographical position, situated at the junction of two continents and right at the gates of a third, gave it extreme importance and influence out of porportions to its size and resources. The space which this mosaic has filled in the picture of the ancient world was a key position, — an important bridge connecting the North with the South, and the East with the West, — the Islands of the Sea with the great empires of Asia. It has been likened to a hub, around which the slow-moving wheel of time revolved.

The Land of Israel (Hebrew: Eretz-Israel) designates what became later "Palestine" (or the "Holy Land") — a name which stems from that of one of Israel's arch enemies — the Philistines.

On the beautiful and fertile Plain of Jezreel-Esdraelon great armies have often wrestled for its control. Here came the Pharaohs, the Hebrews (after the Exodus from Egypt and their inheritance of the Promised Land —Canaan), Joshua, Deborah and Barak fighting against Sisera, Gideon, who with his three hundred braves smote the enemy. Here Saul and Jonathan fell in battle and following came the kingdom of David and the reign of King Solomon who built the Temple in Jerusalem. Then came Xerxes, Sennacherib, Alexander the Great, the Maccabees, the Romans under Titus, the Byzantines, the Arabs from Arabia, the Crusaders under Richard the Lion-hearted, Saladin, the Mamelukes, the Ottoman Turks, Napoleon, the British with General Allenby in World

War I. Here, last of all, is the state of Israel.

The importance of Israel, however, lay not in its transient political power and material wealth, but in its spiritual message to mankind — the Ten Commandments, the Bible and the writings of the Hebrew prophets that gave the world its exalted code of morals.

Here Jewish history began nearly four thousand years ago and despite nearly two thousand years of dispersion the link between the People of Israel and the Land of Israel has never been broken. This little country has given the world two of its great religions, — the Jewish and the Christian — and as consequence, for over two thousand years, has held the interest and affections of increasing numbers spread over the globe. It also occupies a very

9

important place in the religious veneration and thoughts of Islam; and is thus the Holy Land to all these three great faiths.

Unfortunately for the peace of this hub-land, the axle on which this great allegorical wheel turned, was but poorly greased (except with the blood of rival nations) and, to carry the allegory a step further, it frequently ran hot, and seriously burnt the heart of the wheel.

Left: The Coastal
Plain
Center: The Mountain
Range
Right: The Jordan
Rift

RELIEF MAP OF ISRAEL

ISRAEL is a land of striking contrasts, presenting in its relatively restricted area a series of extreme differences in altitude, which roughly divide its surface into three unequal strips running from north to south. This peculiarity is seen at a glance when one looks at a relief map of the country: although this configuration is somewhat distorted in the region of Mt. Carmel and the plain northwest of it. Excluding these last, we have, starting at the Mediterranean seaboard, **firstly**, the Coastal Plain, stretching from the southern spurs of the Lebanon in the north, to the border of Egypt in the south, broken only by the headland of Carmel where it juts out across it to form the Bay of Haifa-Acre.

Secondly, the broad Central Highlands, starting with the southern continuation of the Lebanon in the north; this highland extends with interruption only of a portion of the Plain of Jezreel-Esdraelon, right to the Negev and the desert of northern Sinai. This second strip is cut up into various grades of elevation: namely, the foothills along the Coastal Plain called in their southern portion, the Shephelah, in the Bible. This part of the hill country ranges from 900 to 1800 feet in altitude. Contained in this same zone are several groups of higher mountains; that in the Jerusalem-Hebron region, which is the largest, two or three isolated elevations in Samaria, and similarly in Upper Galilee in the north. Some of these heights reach an altitude of 3000 feet above sea level (Mt. Hermon and Mt. Meiron are higher than this — see below).

Thirdly, the lowlands of the Jordan Valley which form a part of the Great Rift and start below the southern frings of Mt. Hermon, extending in a straight southerly direction down to the Gulf of Eilat (Aqabah). Near the northern extremity of this strip rises the Jordan River in the slopes of Hermon; from a point above sea level in the Huleh Valley, where its three main tributaries unite, the Jordan flows south and enters the Sea of Galilee which is 700 feet below sea level. Further south, the valley attains much greater proportions and continues to broaden as it approaches the Dead Sea As the crow flies, the distance between these two lakes is 65 miles. Here the Jordan, falling very gradually, winds in and out through its marl bed, to enter the Dead Sea at 1290 feet below sea level.

The Holy Land in Roman times

At Jericho, the low plain is about 18 miles wide, and in the Dead Sea region it is almost entirely filled by the lake, a body of water 47 miles long by 9 miles wide. This breadth is irregularly increased by coastal plains of varying proportions, insignificant except for that of the "Lashon" (the "Tongue" — El-Lisan in Arabic) peninsula, which stretches about three quarters of the way across the lake. The eastern and western sides of the valley, or depression, rise abruptly to the high mountains bordering either side of it. The Dead Sea occupies the greatest depth, 1310 feet deep. The immense chasm of the Jordan and Dead Sea Valley is a unique geological phenomenon which possesses the additional, remarkable feature of having no outlet to the sea for the great volume of water that flows into it as the drainage of vast areas around it. This fact is caused by the obstruction continued by the mountain ridge which crosses the Arabah (Aravah) Valley to the south of it.

The Jordan Valley and the maritime slopes of Israel present a great variety of climate, soil, flora and fauna. The climate is cool in the hills and definitely tropical in the deep depression of the Jordan. The range and distribution of air temperature place Israel as a whole in the sub-tropical belt, though areas like the Jordan Valley and the Dead Sea experience tropical heat, and high mountain elevations enjoy the coolness of a temperate climate. Freezing is not uncommon in Jerusalem in winter, but snow is infrequent and rarely lasts more than a day or two. To the north, heavier snowfalls occur, and on Mt. Hermon perpetual snow lies on the protected flanks of the peak.

In ancient Hebrew lore, the year was divided into only two seasons — the autumn and spring season of the rain, and the season of the sun, for there are no distinct transition periods. Rainfall is generous in the highlands during the winter but is light in the Negev, in the lower part of the Jordan

Valley and in the Sinai Peninsula, where it drops to 5 inches (20 m"ms) and less per year. Rainfall in these regions is irregular so that droughts may occur today as they did in ancient times. During the summer season, as a rule, there is no rain from the end of April to November. In October, after

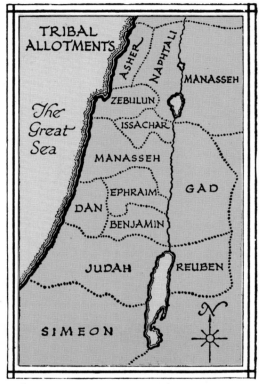

a long, dry season the land is thirsty and ready to drink the blessings of heaven.

Altitude of places in Israel: Mt. St. Catherine in Sinai = 8,718 feet, Mt. Hermon = 9,101 feet, Mt. Meiron (near Zefat-Safed) = 3,986 feet, Rosh-Ramon in the Negev = 3,415 feet, Zefat (Safed) = 3,168 feet, Jerusalem = 2,739 feet, Mt. Tabor = 1,940 feet, Mt. Carmel (highest point) = 1,801 feet, Haifa (city's upper residential area) = 990 feet, Beer-Sheva = 792 feet, Tel-Aviv = 99 feet - all above sea level. Below sea level are: Sodom (Dead Sea area) = 1,303 feet (lowest point on earth), Tiberias = 693 feet, Jericho = 825 feet.

Total area of Israel before the Six Day War in 1967 was 7,922 sq. miles. Population (May 1979) = 3,750,000 (including 600,000 non-Jews). Total area, including the Administrated Areas within the Cease-fire lines, is 34,593 sq. miles, plus almost a million Arabs (and others) now added to the total population, living in Samaria, Judea, the Gaza Strip, Sinai and the Golan Heights.

ISRAEL is the land of the Bible and the names of the Twelve Tribes are: **Reuben, Simeon, Levi, Judah, Dan, Naphtali, Gad, Asher, Issachar, Zebulun, Joseph (later Ephraim and Manasseh) and Benjamin.** Each of the Twelve Tribes, with the exception of Levi, received inheritance in the Promised Land (See page 57).

SHALOM שלום

A **"Sabra"** (Heb. "Tzabar" for Cactus) is a person born in Israel. The "all purpose" word of greeting is **SHALOM**, which means peace (Arabic: Salam), and, "We shall meet again" in Hebrew is **LE-HIT-RA-OT!**

Types of settlement in Israel, other than cities and towns, are : the MOSHAVA (Pl. Moshavot) a colony, a rural settlement, where the farms are the private property of the settler. The first to be established was Petach-Tikva ("Doorway of hope") east of Tel-Aviv, 1875.

The KIBBUTZ (Pl. Kibbutz'im) a collective, communal settlement where all members live and work together, each working to his ability and receiving equally all his needs. No salaries are paid to the members and money is not in use within the settlement. Members receive annually a small amount of money to be spent when on vacation. Similar to the Kibbutz is the KEVUTZA (Pl. Kevutz'ot). First Kibbutz, Deganya in the Jordan Valley, 1910.

The **Moshav,** (Pl. Moshav'im) a small-holders settlement where every settler lives with his family and tills a plot of land leased to him by the Jewish National Fund, is not entitled to engage hired labour and where, mutual help, cooperative purchase and sales are basic principles. First Moshav was Nahalal in the Jezre'el Valley, 1920.

In use in Israel are Kilometers, not miles (1 mile = 1.6 Kilometer). Land is measured by Dunams (1 Acre = 4 Dunams). Temperature is in centigrade (see Temperature Equivalents); weights are in Kilograms (1 Kilogram = 2.2 pounds); lengths are in meters (1 meter = 3.3 feet); 1 meter = 100 centimeter and 1 inch = 2.5 cm. The electric current is 220 AC single phase, 50 cycles, and the Israel "Pound" or "Lira" (Pl. "Lirot" or I.L.) has 100 Agora Coins are 1, 5, 10 and 25 Agora, ½ and 1 "Lira", and notes — 5, 10, 50, 100 and 500 "Lirot". A telephone token is an "Asimon" (for local calls from street booths or post offices).

TEMPERATURE EQUIVALENTS

cent.		fahr.	cent.		fahr.
0	—	32	27	—	81
10	—	50	28	—	82
15	—	59	29	—	84
16	—	61	30	—	86
17	—	63	31	—	88
18	—	64	32	—	90
19	—	66	33	—	91
20	—	68	34	—	93
21	—	70	35	—	95
22	—	72	36	—	97
23	—	73	37	—	99
24	—	75	38	—	100
25	—	77	39	—	102
26	—	79	40	—	104

Kilometers (K"m) to Miles (Mls.)

K"m	=	Mls.	K"m	=	Mls.
8	=	5	48	=	30
16	=	10	64	=	40
24	=	15	80	=	50
32	=	20	90	=	56,4
40	=	25	100	=	63,5

SAY IT IN HEBREW

S'licha	— Excuse (me)	Ken	— Yes	En Li	— I have'nt
Beva'kasha	— Please	Loe	— No	Eifoh?	— Where?
Todah (Rabah)	— Thanks (very much)	Ein Davar	— Never mind	Yafeh	— Nice
Boker Tov	— Good Morning	Mayim	— Water	Gadol	— Big, large
Erev Tov	— Good evening	Le'chayim	— To life!	Kattan	— Small
Laila Tov	— Good night	Mazal Tov	— Good luck!	Be'yoker	— Expensive
Kessef	— Money	Hag Same'ach	— Happy holiday!	Be'zoll	— Cheap
		Yesh Li	— I have	Metzu'yan	— Splendid

Ain (or Ein)	— Spring	Har	— Mountain	Nahal	— Brook
Be'er	— Well	Giv'ah	— Hill	Nahar	— River
Beth (or Beit)	— House	Ramah	— Height	Mappal	— Fall (Wat.)
Derekh	— Way	Tell	— Mound	Sha'ar	— Gate
Emek	— Valley	Hof	— Coast/Beach	Ya'ar	— Forest
Eretz	— Land	K'far	— Village	Yam	— Sea
Nof	— View	Migdal	— Tower	Agam	— Lake
Gan	— Garden	Tira	— Castle	Rehov	— Street

GENERAL INFORMATION

POSTS, TELEGRAMS AND TELEPHONE

Main post offices in Israel are open Sunday to Thursday — 8 A.M. to 6 P.M. Fridays and holiday eves — 8 A.M. to 2 P.M. Some branches close between 12.30 and 3.30 P.M.

Post offices are closed on Saturdays and holidays, but central telegraph offices in main post offices are open day and night, seven days a week, for cables and international phone calls.

BUSINESS AND SHOPPING HOURS

Shopping hours are generally as follows: 8.30 A.M. — 1 P.M.; 4 P.M. — 7 P.M. Fridays and holiday eve — 8.30 A.M. until early afternoon.

Banks are open: Sunday to Thursday — 8.30 A.M. to 12.30 P.M. (closed Wednesday P.M.); Friday and holiday eves — 8.30 — 12 noon.

KEEPING "KOSHER"

All hotels and most restaurants in Israel (except for the non-Jewish ones) keep "Kosher" and observe the Jewish dietary laws: No butter or milk before, with, or after meat; no non-Kosher dishes, no fire or cooking and no smoking (in dining halls) on the Sabbath. The "regular" Shalom greeting changes to "Shabbat Shalom" on the Sabbath, and "Hag-Same'akh" (Happy Holiday) on holidays.

Public transport (regular buses and trains) does not operate; banks, government and public institutions, shops, offices and places of entertainment (theatres and cinemas) are closed on the Sabbath and on religious and national holidays.

Moslem and Christian establishments close on Friday and Sunday respectively.

TIME CONVERTER

ISRAEL	8 A.M.	NOON	4 P.M.	8 P.M.	MDNT
France/Germany	7 A.M.	11 A.M.	3 P.M.	7 P.M.	11 P.M.
England	6 A.M.	10 A.M.	2 P.M.	6 P.M.	10 P.M.
Rio de Janeiro	3 A.M.	7 A.M.	11 A.M.	3 P.M.	7 P.M.
Washington/N.Y.	1 A.M.	5 A.M.	9 A.M.	1 P.M.	5 P.M.
L.A./S. Francisco	10 P.M.	2 A.M.	6 A.M.	10 A.M.	2 P.M.
Melbourne	4 P.M.	8 P.M.	MDNT	4 A.M.	8 A.M.
Japan	3 P.M.	7 P.M.	11 P.M.	3 A.M.	7 A.M.
Moscow	9 A.M.	1 P.M.	5 P.M.	9 P.M.	1 A.M.

JERUSALEM

Beautiful for situation, the joy of the whole earth is Mount Zion, on the sides of the north, The city of the great King... Walk about Zion, and go round about her, Tell the towers thereof, Mark ye well her bulwarks, consider her palaces; That ye may tell it to the generation following. Ps. 48:3, 13

THE OLD CITY OF JERUSALEM

Detail from AMIR'S Pictorial map — 1976

Pray for the peace of Jerusalem: they shall prosper that love thee.

Peace be within thy walls, and prosperity within thy palaces. (Ps. 122; 6, 7)

The "Knesset" (Parliament) Building

JERUSALEM is the capital of the state of Israel, the seat of the government and the "Knesset", which is Israel's "Parliament". The city was again united after the Six Day War in 1967 and has today a population of about 384,000 (May 1979) of which, about 284,000, mostly Jews, live in the new city and about 100,000 in Eastern Jerusalem including the old city, of which the majority (approx. 88,000) are Moslems, with a minority (approx. 12,500) of Christians of various denominations.

The name Jerusalem has often been translated as city of peace, assuming that it originated from the Hebrew Ir Shalom. A holy city for Jews, Christians and Moslems, the story of Jerusalem is undoubtedly one of the most moving and dramatic chapters in the annals of history.

It was the capital, for almost four centuries, of the Kings of Israel and Judah, from David and Solomon to Jehoiachin and Zedekiah; and it was the home of the Prophets from Isaiah and Micah to Jeremiah, Habakkuk, Zephaniah, Ezekiel, Haggai and Zechariah.

Jerusalem, capital of Israel and the spiritual and cultural center of the Jewish people the world over, was, after David made it his capital in about 1000 B.C., the center of Jewish sovereignty and faith. It has always been the focus and forum of Jewish religious life and aspiration.

Jerusalem lies on an irregular quadrangle of rock, sloping north-west to south-east, slightly below the watershed of the Judean highland ridge. The "mountains that are round about" (Ps. 125:2) form a triangle whose west side is part of the main

Jerusalem — the Citadel ("David's Tower")

With its massive ramparts, its picturesque moat and glacis, its impregnable towers and crenellated walls, the Citadel is one of the most striking. monuments in the whole city. Our knowledge of the buildings which anciently occupied this locality is derived from the history of Josephus, who wrote in the first century A.D., and had personal knowledge of them. He narrates that Herod the Great built (about 25 B.C.), a magnificent fortified palace here, with fine gardens, extending over a large area. He specially mentions the three massive and lofty towers which Herod built and called Phasaelus, Hippicus and Mariamme. They were named for his brother, friend and wife, respectively.

Judean ridge (c. 2,669 feet at the highest point of the city).

The present wall around the old city was built in the middle of the 16th century by Suleiman The Magnificent. It has eight gates/entrances which are: Zion Gate, at the south-west corner; Jaffa Gate in the west; New Gate, Damascus Gate and Herod's Gate in the north; St. Stephen's (or the Lions Gate), the (closed) Golden Gate in the east and, the Dung Gate in the south. The perfectly preserved circumvallation-wall (length — 2½ miles) stands on the foundations of the walls of Hadrian's square "Aelia Capitolina" (135 A.D.) which, for the first time excluded Mt. Zion and Mt. Ophel and includes remains of other earlier walls — Herod (37 B.C.), Agrippa (41 A.D.), and Saladin (1187).

The Citadel of Jerusalem (near Jaffa Gate) in its present state is the work of Crusaders and Mamelukes incorporating ruins of the heavily fortified Palace of Herod the Great, now called "David's Tower". Excavations within the citadel brought to light the foundations of the Hasmonean city wall.

The old city is divided into four quarters by her two main thoroughfares of stepped, stone-paved streets, too narrow for wheeled traffic. One runs from the Jaffa Gate at the west to the center of the city, where it is intersected by the other, extending from the Damascus Gate on the north. The traditional Via Dolorosa (Way of the Cross) starts at Antonia, near Stephen's (Lions) Gate and ends at the Church of the Holy Sepulchre.

The Western ("Wailing") Wall

The Western Wall is part of the beautifully fashioned masonry walls which surrounded the Temple Area in Herod's (2nd Temple) time. The archaeological excavations near the south-western corner of the Wall are of great interest; as work progressed here in recent years, more and more became·known of the nature of the high supporting walls, almost 15 feet thick, of the Temple Mount built by Herod, of its superb plan and of the extent of its preservation in its various sections. The excavations are sponsored by the Israel Exploration Society and the Institute of Archaeology of the Hebrew University, directed by Prof. B. Mazar, with the extensive assistance of Meir Ben-Dov.

THE WESTERN ("Wailing") WALL

(Hebrew: Kotel-Hama'aravi), the holiest shrine of the Jewish world, is a continuation of the western wall surrounding the ancient Temple area enclosure. It survives from a very early Temple wall plus upper levels constructed as late as the sixteenth century. Many courses of hewn or unhewn stone lie below the present level of the wall, the lowest resting on the Tyropoeon valley bedrock.

The ancient walls of Jerusalem: First Wall — time of King Solomon. Second Wall — probably first built by Hezekiah (2 Chron. 32:5) and then rebuilt by Nehemiah (445 B.C.). Third Wall — (or Agrippa's Wall) 41 A.D.

The history of the Temple Area is the history of Jerusalem. Its main dates, viz: the construction of the First Temple by Solomon in about 950 B.C., its destruction by Nebuchadnezzar in 586 B.C., the erection of the Second Temple in about 520 B.C. and of Herod's splendid Temple in 10 B.C. to be destroyed in 70 A.D.

THE CHRISTIAN PERIOD begins in the 33rd year of Herod's reign (5 B.C.), when Jesus was born in Bethlehem, about five miles south of Jerusalem. The ministry of Jesus — in which period of His life He spent a considerable time in the Holy City — commenced about the year 27 A.D. The visits of Jesus to Jerusalem, as listed in the New Testament, were: His presentation by Mary and Joseph (Luke 2: 22-39); His visit as a boy of 12 (Luke 2:41-50); His Passover visit as in John 2:13-22; His Sojourn identified

Jerusalem — Church of the Holy Sepulchre

The interior consists of two principal parts: the Domed Circular Building on the west, which covers the tomb, and the Rectangular Church on the east. Immediately after entering (on the right), a steep staircase ascends to the chapels on Golgotha or Mt. Calvary. Low in the altarspace of the main central apse on the east, a round opening marks the place where the Cross of Christ stood in the Crucifixion, fastened in the rock. On the floor, near the main entrance, is the Stone of Unction, upon which the body of Jesus is said to have been anointed by Nicodemus (John 19:39). Beneath the dome, in the center of the rotunda, is the Chapel of the Holy Sepulchre, consisting of two chambers: first, the Chapel of the Angel, in the center of which is a stone said to be the one which closed the door of the tomb, which was rolled away by the angel. Through a low door the Chapel of the Sepulchre is entered; the Tomb of Christ is on the right hand side, covered with a marble slab. It is 5 feet long, 2 feet wide and 3 feet high.

by the curing of the cripple at the Pool of Bethesda (John 5); His last visit to Jerusalem, from Palm Sunday to Good Friday (Mark 11-16 and parallels) in which He is recorded as being in an "Upper room" (Mark 14: 15); the Garden of Gethsemane (Mark 14:32); the palace of Caiaphas (John 18:22-24); the Praetorium (John 18: 28); Gabbatha (John 19:13) and Golgotha (Matt. 27:33; Mark 15:22; John 19:17,41; Heb. 13:12).

THE CHURCH OF THE HOLY SEPULCHRE or of **The Resurrection** has for over sixteen centuries been venerated as perhaps the holiest Christian shrine on the face of the earth, having since the days of the Emperor Constantine marked the site of the **Tomb of Christ** and of **Golgotha** ("Place of Skull" — John 19:17), or **Calvary** (Luke 23:33), which was the place of His Crucifixion.

The identification of these holy sites

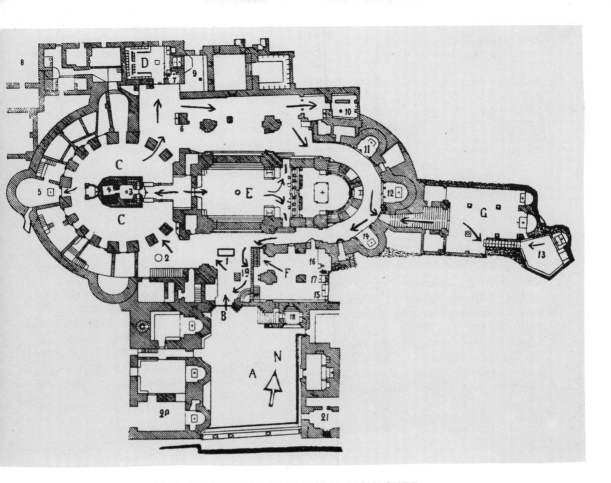

THE CHURCH OF THE HOLY SEPULCHRE

A. Courtyard

B. Main entrance to the church

C. The Rotunda

D. Chapel of the Apparition

E. Greek Orthodox Cathedral (Catholicon)

F. Golgotha

G. Chapel of St. Helena

1. Stone of Unction

2. Place where the three Marys stood

3. Chapel of the Angel

4. The Holy Sepulchre

5. St. Nicodemus Chapel

6. Altar of St. Mary Magdalene

7. Flagellation column

8. Franciscan convent

9. Franciscan Sacristy

10. Prison of Christ

11. Chapel of Longinus

12. Division of the Vestments

13. Grotto of the Finding of the Holy Cross

14. Crowning with Thorns

15. Chapel of the Nailing to the Cross

16. Greek Orthodox Calvary

17. Altar of Mater Dolorosa

18. Chapel of Agony

19. Chapel of Adam and Altar of Melchizedek

20. The Orthodox Cathedral of St. James

21. St. Abraham Monastery

was accepted by archaeologists and is adhered to by all Latin and Oriental Orthodox Christians. This most historic church of Christendom was begun by Constantine following the pilgrimage to the Holyland of his mother Helena in the early 4th century.

Bishop Mecarius of Jerusalem, acting under Constantine's directions, searched and found the tomb of Christ and Golgotha in 325 A.D., and upon these two sites the Emperor built two magnificent churches, that of **Anastasis**, or Resurrection, over the tomb and the **Martyrion** on the place where the three crosses were found.

The German **Erloeser Kirche**, church of the Redeemer stands a few hundred yards south-east of the church of the Holy Sepulchre. When Jerusalem was taken by the Crusaders, the new **Order of the Hospitallers**, or Knights of St. John, was founded and they erected hospices and other buildings in this part. In 1216 the Hospitallers church was converted into a hospital under the name of **Muristan**, from which the area took its name.

THE **"VIA DOLOROSA"** proper, begins at the Crusader Chapel of the "Crowning with Thorns", north of the Temple area. Near it, within **Ecce Homo Convent of the Dames de Zion** are some of the most important ancient monuments — the "Lithostratos", the square of the Antonia Fortress and the Ecce Homo Arch. Here, the good nuns-sisters are exemplary guides and explain their sacred sites in a manner, which combines edification with exact science.

Closeby is the Franciscan Convent of the Flagellation and further east, close to St. Stephen's (or the Lions) Gate, are the Pools of Bethesda (John 5:2) and the most beautiful, perfectly preserved, Crusader church of St. Anne, at the French Monastery of the White Fathers.

Via Dolorsa: See Page 35.

The Via Dolorosa

The Dome of the Rock (Mosque of Omar)

THE ARAB Conquest of Jerusalem occurred in 637 A.D. when, after a siege of a few months the city surrendered to the Caliph Omar 'a wise and just leader'. Omar, who was the first successor to the Prophet Mohammed's leadership, found and cleared the Sacred Rock in the Temple Area and erected thereon a temporary place of worship. When the Ommyad Caliph Abd El-Malek, whose capital was Damascus, came to power, it suited his policy to establish a center of worship and pilgrimage in his territory to serve as a counterpoise to the prestige and political influence which the Holy places of Mecca and Medina gave to Abdalla, the rival Caliph. Accordingly he determined to build a Mosque in Jerusalem, on the site of the Temple of Solomon, surpassing in grandeur any sanctuary to be found in all Islam. So he built, in 691 A.D., the renowned Dome of the Rock (commonly called the Mosque of Omar) on the site of Omar's place of worship.

The Temple Area, Mt. Moriah or Temple Mount, is occupied chiefly by the **Haram Esh-Sherif,** the Noble Sanctuary — also called the Mosque of Omar, from the most famous of its shrines. Mt. Moriah is first mentioned in the book of Genesis (Gen. 22 : 1—4) when the Patriarch Abraham was directed to go up to the "land of Moriah" to "one of the mountains" which God will point out and there offer up his sacrifice.

When the Caliph Omar entered Jerusalem he constructed a place of temporary worship upon the Sacred Rock which he identified as the place from which the Prophet Mohammed made his Ascension to heaven. On the site thus chosen, the Ommyad Caliph 'Abd el-Malek built the Dome of the Rock in the year 691.

South of the Dome of the Rock with its golden dome, stands another (silver dome) Mosque called El Aksa, meaning "the distant", which refers to the fact that this is the most distant sanctuary visited by Mohammed. Only the Ka'aba in Mecca is held in greater sanctity. Most authorities concur that Justinian's Basilica, built in 550 or earlier, in honour of St. Mary, stood here, and that parts of the present Mosque date from that building.

23

Above: The Dome of the Rock — Moslems at prayer
Below: The Dome of the Rock — interior

Mount Zion

King David's Tomb

The Citadel — interior

Jaffa Gate near the Citadel

MOUNT ZION

The high plateau (2564 feet), on which the old, the historical Jerusalem stands, is a triangle between the valleys of Kidron and Hinnom in the east and west respectively. A third shallow valley, the ancient Tyropoeon, bisects the triangle, pointing to the south. The two promontories, thus formed, were part of the city until its destruction by Titus. Hadrian, rebuilding Jerusalem as the square Roman city "Aelia Capitolina", excluded the two ridges from the circumvallation. The western ridge is called Mt. Zion and the eastern Mt. Ophel.

A group of buildings south of the Dormitio property are known as the "Prophet David" and also called the **Coenaculum**, or the **Chamber of the Last Supper**. These buildings formerly belonged to the Franciscan Order, which was established here as early as 1333. Gradually their property was encroached upon by the Moslems, who, in 1477 entirely supplanted them. The generally accepted tradition located the "House of John, called Mark" with the "Upper Room" (of the Last Supper), the place where Mary spent the rest of her life and where the Pentecost Miracle took place, on Mt. Zion. This house, as tradition has it, escaped the Roman destruction of Jerusalem and the early Christians installed their first church here. The Byzantines built on this post their **Hagia Zion** — the Mother of Churches, where besides many other pilgrim sites, the Room of the Last Supper, or "Coenaculum", was shown in the south-eastern corner of the church. Under the Coenaculum was the Room of the Washing of the Feet. The place where Mary "fell into eternal sleep", the Dormitio, was located in a crypt in the north-eastern corner.

The Jewish traveller, Benjamin of Tudela, who visited Jerusalem in 1163, then under the Crusaders, introduced the legend to Jewish folklore: "On Mt. Zion are the sepulchres of the House of David and those of the kings who reigned after him..." With their holiest shrine, the Western ("Wailing") Wall being inaccessible to Jews from 1948 to 1967, and with Mt. Zion being the only part of the old city plateau held by Israel after the 1948 war, King David's Tomb on Mt. Zion has been (and continues to be) a hallowed site.

Room of the Last Supper

KING DAVID'S .TOMB is entered through a large vaulted hall now used as a synagogue. The adjoining room shows traces of a decoration of fine, old Armenian tiles. The mighty sarcophagus is covered by an embroidered shroud. An apse, belonging to the Crusader church has been discovered immediately behind it. The Tomb, with fine Torah Crowns standing on the shrouded sarcophagus, is impressive in the scintillation of many candles and oil lamps.

THE COENACULUM, or the **CHAMBER OF THE LAST SUPPER**, entered from a terrace through one of the original windows in the north, is a fine Gothic hall, the pointed arches of which rest on two center columns and on pillars, built into the walls. A stone near the north wall marks the Seat of Christ, and under the central window is a Moslem prayer-niche.

THE DORMITIO ABBEY is the most imposing shrine on Mt. Zion. It was built in Romanesque style at the beginning of the century. The church stands on land which was acquired by the German Emperor during his visit to the country in 1893.

ST. PETER IN GALLICANTE (Cock-crowing) church is a few hundred yards down the hill in the east. It belongs to the Roman Catholic order of The Assumptionists, stands on the site of the ancient Byzantine church of St. Peter and built on the traditional site of the Palace of Caiaphas, where Jesus was judged by the High Priest on the eve of Good Friday.

26

Model of Jerusalem at Holyland Hotel grounds — partial views

The Garden Tomb — Jerusalem

Now in the place where he was crucified there was a garden; and in the garden a new sepulchre, wherein was never man yet laid. There laid they Jesus therefore because of the Jews' preparation day; for the sepulchre was nigh at hand. John 19:41-42

Skull Hill (Golgotha)

THE GARDEN TOMB is reached by a lane, north of Damascus Gate. The property was acquired in 1894, when a Society was formed "For the preservation of the Tomb and Garden outside the walls of Jerusalem, believed by many people to be the Sepulchre and Garden of Joseph of Arimathea". The garden lies on the west side of the prominent hill just outside the city wall, at the foot of the rocky cliff. The rock-cut Tomb, first discovered in 1867, and later excavated, dates from the Roman period and is thought to have been the Tomb belonging to Joseph of Arimathea, of which we read in John 19:41—42. Among the earliest adherents to the belief that this was the Sepulchre of Christ was General Gordon (1882) who was a Bible student as well as a notable British soldier. The garden is a quiet and pleasant spot, lying at the foot of the tomb-covered green hill, just without the city wall, a congenial place for quiet meditation. The rounded hill has a resemblance of the human skull.*

CALVARY, the place of Christ's Crucifixion, is mentioned in Luke 23:33. It is the *Kranion* (meaning "skull") of the original Greek New Testament, whence *"Golgotha"* (from Aramaic for "skull") (Matt. 27:33; John 19:17). *"Calvary"* is derived from the Latin Calvaria. It was near a highway (Matt. 27:39) and "without the gate" (Heb. 13:12).

The Tomb of Christ — at the Garden Tomb

THE MOUNT OF OLIVES (Heb: Har Hazeitim; Ol'ivet 2 Sam. 15:30), "a Sabbath day's journey" from Jerusalem (Acts 1:12), is the most conspicuous landmark of the Holy City. It lies close to the city on the east (Ezek. 11:23), separated from its plateau by the deep, narrow cleft of the Kidron Valley and occupies a dominating position in relation to it. It is about 2930 feet above the Mediterranean, frequently mentioned in connection with the wars and sieges and closely intertwined with the history of Jerusalem

The most comprehensive and finest views of Jeursalem and its unsurpassed panorama are those to be obtained from the Mount of Olives and from its northernmost end — Mt. Scopus, on which are the British War Cemetery, the old Hadassah hospital and Hebrew University. From these points of vantage the visitor, seeing the Holy City for the first time, gets a clear idea of the lay of the land and can form a correct acquaintance with the hills on which the city stands. The ancient city wall can be seen for most of its extent and some of the city gates. Looking eastward, the range of views of the Jordan Valley and of the Dead Sea, with the blue line of the mountains of Moab beyond it, are truely unique, — views which linger with the beholder through life.

The Mount of Olives, occasionally mentioned in the Old Testament, comes into great prominence in New Testament times; on its slope, facing Mount Moriah and the Temple Area lies the largest and oldest Jewish cemetery in the world. It is believed that here will take place the Resurrection of the Dead at the end of time; "Behold the Day of the Lord cometh... and His feet shall stand in that day upon the Mount of Olives which is before Jerusalem..." (Zechariah 14:1,4). It was Jesus' custom to go to the Mount of Olives at evening (John 7:53, 8:1), from here he viewed the city and beheld its stately walls, its strong towers and its magnificent

The Place of Ascension

Temple and here he pronounced his lament over its impending doom and the judgement of its people (Matt. 23:37, 24:3). On the slopes of this mount Jesus taught his prayer (Luke 11:1—4) to his Disciples — an event memorialized here by the chapel on whose walls the Lord's Prayer is written in 35 languages. From the hilltop village of Bethphage Jesus rode a colt down the steep slope, across the Kidron and up the escarpment to walled Jerusalem, entering at an opening that for centuries was said to be the Golden Gate in the east wall (Matt. 21:1—12). After the Last Supper in the Upper Room he retired into the quiet Garden of Gethsemane at its foot, where he was arrested. Tradition places the spot of the Ascension also on the Mount of Olives.

The striking landmark of the Mount of Olives is the tall tower of the Ascension at the Russian Orthodox church. The Latin Ascension Chapel occupies the center of an octagonal courtyard, formed by the ruins of the

Gethsemane and the Mt. of Olives

Gethesmane — Church of All Nations

medieval Ascension church which open to the sky like the Rotunda of the Holy Sepulchre. The bases of the wall-pillars still exist and serve on Ascension Day as altars for the Armenians, Copts and Syrians, while the Catholics celebrate Mass in the central edicule, under the open dome of which a foot-print of Christ is shown. The property here belongs to the Moslems. The Latin property on the Mount of Olives encloses the traditional sites where the Lord's Prayer was taught — the Carmelite convent of Pater-Noster.

GETHSEMANE. The three sections of the Garden of Gethsemane — Franciscan, Armenian and Russian are on the lower reaches of the Mount of Olives, marked today by a few ancient olive, palm and other trees. The church of Gethsemane, correctly called the Basilica of The Agony, is on the south side of the garden. This magnificent new church of All Nations was completed in 1925. Its ceiling consists of twelve shallow domes, each of which is a beautiful panel of glowing mosaics, gifts of the following countries: 1. The Column of the Flagellation — Argentine, 2. St. Veronica's Handkerchief — Chili, 3. The Three Spikes — Brazil, 4. The Shield of St. Francis — Mexico, 5. This being right above the "Rock of Agony" and the High Altar, is the most important one and represents Heaven, with the angels, Old Testament symbols and the four Evangelists — Italy, 6. The Chalice, symbolical of the Sacrament — France, 7. The Holy Cross — Spain, 8. The Holy Sepulchre — England, 9. The Crown of Thorns — Belgium, 10. The One-piece Garment — Canada, 11. The Spear and Sponge — Germany, 12. The Crusader Cross of the Holy Land — The United States.

THE church of The Virgin is near Gethsemane, off the main Jericho road. It stands below the level of the road and is approached by a flight of 15 broad, well-worn steps. Here the legend says that the Mother of Christ was interred by the Apostles. The first church to be built here was that of the first half of the fifth century.

Jerusalem — the Garden of Gethsemane

Gethsemane (Heb. Gat-Shemanim, meaning oil press), A place (Matt. 26:36, Mark 14:32) frequented by Jesus on the slope of the Mount of Olives across the Kidron Valley. Olive trees of great age, the proximity of the Jerusalem city wall and the Kidron Valley ravine, add to the record of the events which took place here an increased vividness.

The magnificent church of Gethsamene, correctly called The Basilica of The Agony lies on the southern side of the Garden. The beautiful facade is in the Byzantine style, consisting of a very attractive open portico fronted with beautiful columns, and between them are large marble statues of the four Evangelists — Matthew, Mark, Luke and John.

Church of All Nations — interior

אם אשכחך ירושלים תשכח ימיני

If I forget thee, O Jerusalem, Let my right hand forget her cunning!

*THE OLD CITY: JERUSALEM WITHIN THE WALLS

*THE OLD, HISTORIC CITY OF JERUSALEM —
EXCURSION AROUND THE CITY WALLS

THE OLD CITY: JERUSALEM WITHIN THE WALLS

In describing the old city, the four quarters, coinciding with its hills, Zion, Acra, Moriah and Bezetha are treated separately (see Mt. Zion & Excursion around the city walls). Commencing with Mount Zion, the southwestern hill, **THE ZION QUARTER** is mainly the Armenian and old Jewish portion of the city.

Entering the square near Jaffa Gate, **David Street** leads down east — a narrow and generally thronged market street — to the Western ("Wailing") Wall and Temple Area. A second road, **Zion Street**, turns out of the square to the south and through the Armenian Quarter leads to the Zion Gate. The ancient **Church of St. James** at the great Armenian Monastery is both interesting and handsome. In an oriental way, it is perhaps the handsomest church in Jerusalem. The walls of the interior are covered with beautiful old tiles to a height of six feet. Above hang large paintings, over 500 years old. The nave is richly ornamented and contains the traditional episcopal throne of St. James the son of Zebedee. In the northern aisle is shown the cell where he was beheaded, by order of Herod (Acts 12:2). In the southeastern corner are shown three stones, taken respectively from Mt. Sinai, Mt. Tabor and from the Jordan, at the place where the Israelites crossed. The Monastery is also the residence of the Patriarch.

Passing through the archway, the street continues to the Zion Gate. Here one road turns to the north, parallel with Zion Street and continues to the Jewish Quarter, and another goes to the east, outside the gate and along the city wall to the Dung Gate. Outside the Zion Gate, and opposite it, is the Armenian Monastery of Mt. Zion which stands on the traditional site of the house of Caiaphas.

THE JEWISH QUARTER (Heb. Ha'rovah Ha'yehudi) was very badly damaged and mostly destroyed during Israel's War of Independence in 1948. Following the siege and the surrender of its small community many of its famous, ancient, historic synagogues and institutions were demolished. Among them were: The Karaites synagogue, the Old Hurvah synagogue of the Ashkenazi Jews which was built in 1864, at whose courtyard was the religious school of Etz Haim, the Yohanan Ben Zakai synagogue, belonging to the Sepharadic Jews, the Tiferet Israel Synagogue which was built in 1872 by Rabbi Nisan Bak. Large scale repair and rebuilding work has been in progress since the Six Day War in 1967.

ACRA, the northwestern hill, is the **Christian Quarter** of Jerusalem, although a considerable part of Zion is occupied by the Armenian section, which is also Christian. The main Christian institutions, including the Church of the Holy Sepulchre, the main Greek and Latin Patriarchates, convents and churches are here.

From the first landing of steps off David's Street, to the left, a lane leads to **The Pool of Hezekiah.** This name to the ancient reservoir, about 220 feet long and 120 feet wide, is from the common belief that it was originally constructed in King Hezekiah's reign, on the assumption that it was the one referred to in the passage, "He made a pool and a conduit and brought water into the city" (2 Kings 20:20). Josephus calls it the **Pool Amygdalon** (Wars 5:9:4). As regards Hezekiah's "pool and conduit", the reader should turn to the description of the Siloam Tunnel.

To the north of David's street is the Convent of St. Saviour, commonly called the Latin Convent, which belongs to the Franciscan Order and is a very large establishment, containing the Church of St. Saviour. Turning to the left, west, one comes to the Greek Convent of St. Theodore on the right, and just beyond it, the Franciscan (Italian) Hospice of Casa Nova.

At the corner formed by the junction of David and Christian streets (about 500 feet from the top of David St.), overlooking the busy market streets, is the Greek Convent of St. John the Baptist. A short distance from here, to the north, a stepped street leads to the court of the **Church of the Holy Sepulchre** (p. 20), and near the end of this street is the entrance to the Mohammedan Mosque of **Sidna 'Omar**. The region south and southeast of the Church of the Holy Sepulchre is called the **Muristan**. Its original boundaries were Christian St. on the west, the middle part of David St. on the south, and the bazaar street on the east. It is chiefly noted for the Frankish inns, hospitals and churches which were erected here in the Middle Ages; especially those of the Knights of St. John (p. 22).

Returning to Christian St. we follow it to its northern end where it is joined by St. Francis St. Descending to the right we reach the main bazaar street of Khan ez-Zeit which follows the bed of the Tyropeon Valley. At this point the Via Dolorosa crosses the Khan ez-Zeit St. and leads past several Stations (which will be described later) down to the main road leading from the Damascus Gate to the Temple Area.

* Zion Street is today called "Omar Ibn El Khattab Street".

MOUNT MORIAH, the Eastern, or Temple Hill is occupied chiefly by the Haram Esh-Sherif, the Noble Sanctuary, — also called the Mosque of Omar. With all the buildings connected with it, it corresponds roughly with the area of the ancient Jewish Temples. The Mosque Area is enclosed on the east and south by the city wall, and on the north and west by buildings and cloisters belonging to the Mosque. This enclosure occupies about one sixth of the walled old city (p. 23). The original "City of David" stood on the southern spur of this hill, and was frequently called Ophel in the Bible. It lies outside and south of the present city wall and of the Temple Area enclosure.

The HILL OF BEZETHA occupies the northeastern quarter of the town, and, broadly speaking, can be said to be bounded on the south by the Via Dolorosa and on the west by the road leading southward from the Damascus Gate. The summit inside the walls is reached at the peak next to the city wall, a little east of the Damascus Gate and above the entrance to Solomon's Quarries. Bezetha is almost entirely the Moslem Quarter of old Jerusalem.

Entering through St. Stephen's (or the Lions) Gate the street goes west and passes, where it is vaulted over, the remains of Herod's **Castle of Antonia**, marked by a massive old ruin with large drafted stones, on the righthand side, although the main part of the fortress is on the left. A little further on is the Franciscan Convent and **Chapel of Scourging**. Adjoining the chapel is the Chapel of Flagellation. At this point the **Via Dolorosa**, or the **Way of The Cross**, along which Christ carried the Cross commences.

THE VIA DOLOROSA

I   In the courtyard of the Castle of Antonia (now El-Omariya school) was formerly the "Chapel of the Crowning with Thorns", and here is placed the **1st Station of the Cross.**

II   The **2nd Station**, where the Cross was laid upon Jesus is outside, across the street. Just where the ancient Roman triumphal arch, called the **Arch of Ecce Homo** crosses the road, is the **Convent of the Sisters of Zion.** The main vault stands over the road, while the northern side-arch is seen in the choir of the beautiful Church of the Sisters of Zion. The remains of the heavy Roman **pavement** are to be seen, to the full extent of the span of the arches, and extending far to the north of them, in the lower vaults of the convent, lying several feet below the level of the present road; in it are seen several games cut in the flags, for the amusement of the soldiers. This pavement, which is a section of the Roman street, is thought to be the **"Gabbatha"**, or the "pavement", called the **Lithostratos** in Greek.

III   Outside the Armenian Hospice, on the Damascus Gate road (or "King Solomon"), is a broken column in the wall, which marks the **3rd Station of the Cross** where Jesus fell under the weight of the Cross.

IV   The Way of the Cross follows this street southward, and a second slab in the wall not many steps further on, marks the **4th Station**, where Jesus met His mother.

V   Further on, at the turning of the Via Dolorsa to the right, is the **5th Station**; here Simon the Cyrenian took the Corss from Christ.

VI   The street now goes westward, and a few hundred feet further up is the **6th Station**; where St. Veronica wiped the sweat from her Lord's face.

VII   A little further on we cross the main bazaar street of Khan ez-Zeit; and just here is the **7th Station** called **Porta Judiciara**, through which gate Christ is said to have left the town on His way to Calvary.

VIII   Passing the German Hospice of St. John, on the left, we notice a black Cross in the wall of the Greek Convent, which marks the **8th Station**; here, it is said, Jesus spoke to the women who followed and lamented for him.

IX   The Via Dolorosa proper comes to an end here, although the **9th Station** is shown in the Coptic Monastery, east of the Church of the Holy Sepulchre, where the weight of the Cross caused Jesus again to fall down.

    The 10th, 11th, 12th and 13th Stations are on Calvary, in the Church of the Holy Sepulchre; the 14th and last, is the Holy Sepulchre itself;

X   Calvary: Jesus is stripped of His garments.

XI   Calvary: Jesus is nailed to the Cross.

XII   Jesus dies on the Cross.

XIII   Jesus body is taken from the Cross.

XIV   Holy Sepulchre: Jesus body is laid in the Tomb of Joseph of Arimathea.

TOPOGRAPHY

JERUSALEM stands on a group of two (subdivided into four) hills, which form a spur of the main Judean range, lying just below and east of the watershed. These hills are surrounded on the west, south and east by deep ravines, or valleys with precipitous sides, while the northern approach is comparatively level and is the quarter from which Jerusalem has usually been attacked. This enclosed area is highest at its northwest corner and has a downward trend toward the southeast.

In ancient times the hills and valleys of Jerusalem were very much more clearly marked than they are now; but the numerous destructions and changes which the city has undergone, and the accumulation of debris through the ages, have filled up the valleys and lowered the heights, giving the place a closer resemblance to an irregular plateau than to a region of prominent hills and deep valleys. It is difficult now to imagine the aspect formerly presented.

The deep central valley, called El Wad (Ha'gai in Hebrew), or the Tyropeon, running roughly from north to south divides Jerusalem into the two main hills: the Eastern and the Western. These two hills are subdivided by an Eastern and a Western Gully into the Western and Northwestern Hills on the one side, and the Northern and Eastern Hills on the other. Of these subdivisions, the Eastern and Western are the most important.

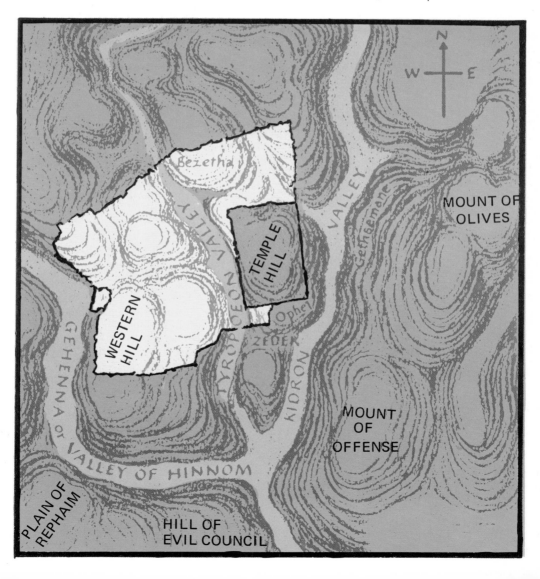

Jerusalem — view from the Mount of Olives

THE WESTERN HILL, now called Mt. Zion, occupies the southwest portion of the town and lies between the central or Tyropeon Valley on the east, the upper part of the Valley of Hinnom on the west, the lower part of Hinnom on the south, and by the western gully (marked by David Street), on the north. In the time of the early kings of Judah the "UPPER CITY" stood here, and it was thought by some that Jebus, of the Canaanites occupied the hill. Mt. Zion is 100 feet higher than Mt. Moriah.

THE NORTH-WESTERN HILL, the so-called Acra, is situated to the north of Mt. Zion, and separated from it by the Western Gully, which is now almost obliterated by debris. Its eastern side falls into the Tyropeon. The greater portion of this hill was not included within the walls until about 40 B.C. On its eastern slopes stands the Church of the Holy Sepulchre.

THE EASTERN HILL, called Mt. Moriah, occupies the southeast portion of Jerusalem and lies between the Kidron Valley on the east, and the Tyropeon on the west, and is bounded on the south by the junction of the two at the Pool of Siloam. The present crest is the Sacred Rock, in the "Dome of the Rock"; but according to some authorities it formerly attained a greater height near the Mosque El Aksa, which is thought to have been cut down by the Maccabees. The correctness of this theory is doubted by many, who look to the escarpment of the rock at the Castle of Antonia for the above cutting. The southern part of the hill was called OPHEL, and is the most ancient portion of the whole city. There stood the "strong-hold of the Jebusites", which David rebuilt and called the "City of David". On Mt. Moriah Solomon built his famous Temple and Palace.

THE NORTHERN HILL, called Bezetha, is bisected by a valley which, having its origin to the northeast, passes by Herod's Gate and the Pool of Bethesda, and joins the Kidron north of the Golden Gate; this latter portion has been filled in or built up. The upper part of the Tyropeon skirts Bezetha on the west.

This hill culminates in the prominence just outside the Damascus Gate, known as Gordon's Calvary (See Garden Tomb — page 29) and the elevated quarter of the town south of it; the long trench between the two being, at least in part, an artificial cutting. Bezetha's southern spur terminated in the lofty rock eminence upon which stood the Tower of Antonia, now occupied by the building housing the school of El-Omariya. The southern portion of Bezetha was incorporated into the city about the time of Nehemiah.

The Kidron Valley and eastern Wall

VALLEYS

THE VALLEY OF HINNOM (Heb. Gei-ben-Hinnom, Arb. Wadi er-Rababeh), lying outside the city, though much encumbered with debris, is less changed than the two other main valleys. It starts west of the city, near the Jaffa Gate, taking first a southerly course, and then swinging east around Mt. Zion; it joins the Tyropeon and Kidron Valleys in the deep gorge on the south (Arb. Wadi en-Nar).

THE KIDRON VALLEY, also outside the city, bounds Jerusalem on its whole eastern extent. It is now greatly changed from its ancient aspect. By the process of filling up, its bottom is not only from 10 to 50 feet higher than it was, but lies 30 feet to the east of its former bed, while the ancient surface of its western side, at the southeast angle of the present city wall is not reached before going through 36 feet of debris.

THE CENTRAL, OR TYROPEON VALLEY, which is historically one of Jerusalem's most important natural features, has suffered most from the manifold wreckage and waste of the city; it has become so chocked with the debris fallen into it from both sides, as to be far less noticeable than anciently, when it formed a very distinct division between the Eastern and Western Hills. Often opposing forces held its two sides. The Tyropeon, sometimes translated the "Cheesemongers Valley", traverses the whole city: starting at the Damascus Gate and pursuing a broadly southward course, it leaves the city near the southeast corner at the Pool of Siloam. Its bed is practically marked by the road from the Damascus to the Dung Gates, and it has been found that from 20 to 90 feet of debris overlies the ancient surface. In ancient times the valley was spanned by two great bridges (one of which was thought to be, until the recent archaeological excavations, "Robinson's Arch"), to connect the upper city with the Temple hill.

THE COURSE OF THE ANCIENT CITY WALLS

Much of the beauty and the history of Jerusalem is in her walls, towers and gates, whose origin is still debated. For the walls to be down was a national calamity; after the sieges of Nebuchadnezzar and Hadrian the capital was practically abandoned. "Build thou the walls of Jerusalem" (Ps. 51:18) was a challenging crv.

THE FIRST WALL OF JERUSALEM may be the ancient rampart (now greatly excavated) built by the Jebusites, captured by David (I Chron. 11:4-8), repaired by him and Joab, and enlarged by Solomon. The wall of David's city was 550 feet south of the present southern wall. Another early Hebrew wall is known to have stretched north-east from the City of David to approximately the south-east corner of the present walls; and another very early wall of uncertain date extended north and south parallel to the Tyropeon Valley at a point near the center of the present southern wall. Other ancient southern walls have been found west of "David's City" which defended the early streets. Solomon, enlarging David's small town, naturally built "the wall of Jerusalem round about" to protect his palaces and Temple (I Kings 3:1, 9:17), paying for it with a levy of taxes (I Kings 9:15). Not only did he build it on the east, but carried it west on the north side of the sacred enclosure, then south along the suburban "Mishneh" or "Second Quarter". The extent of the city on the north and north-west shortly after his time is not known.

Archaeological excavations near corner of eastern and southern walls

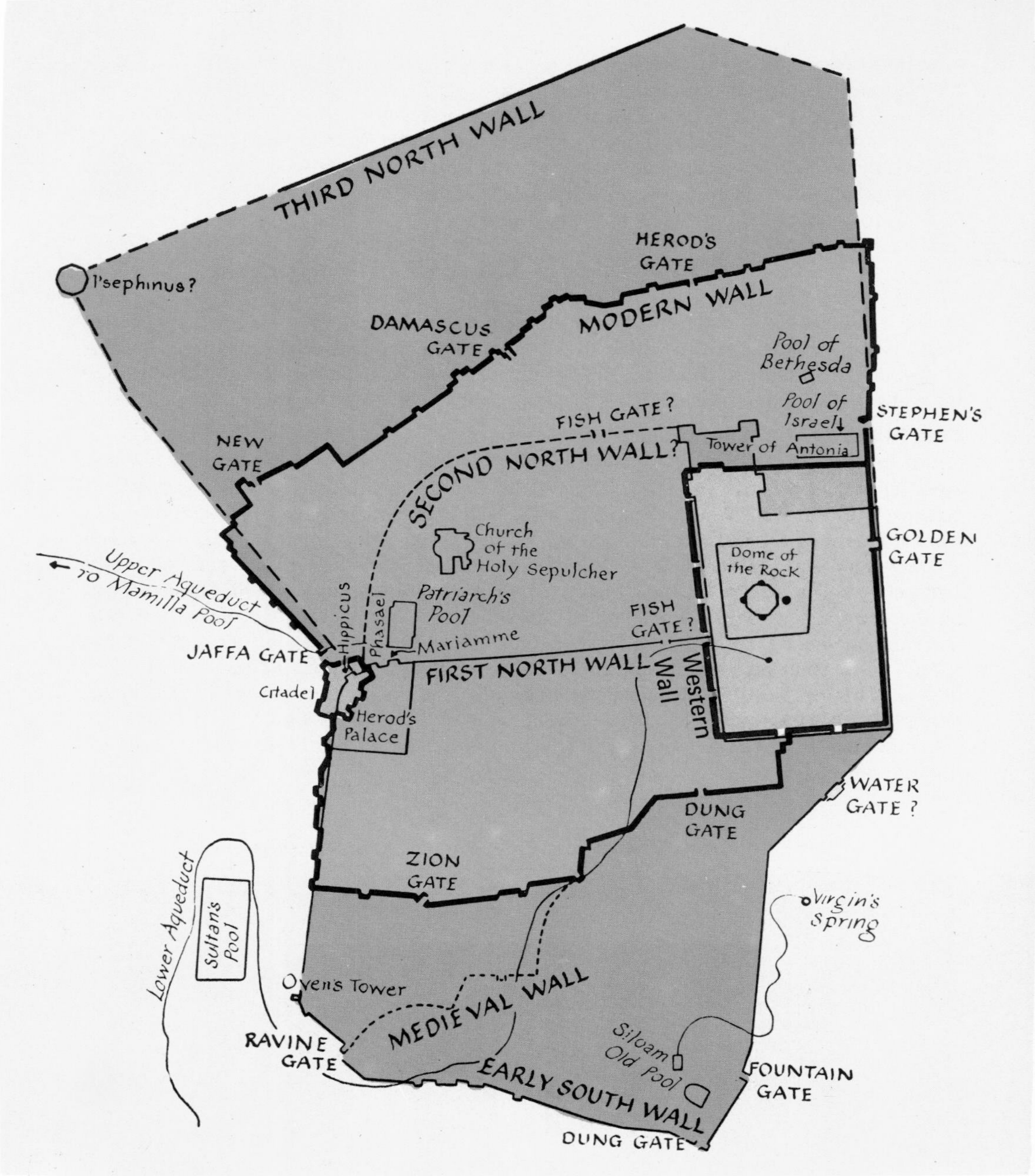
THIRD NORTH WALL
I'sephinus?
HEROD'S GATE
MODERN WALL
DAMASCUS GATE
Pool of Bethesda
Pool of Israel
STEPHEN'S GATE
FISH GATE?
Tower of Antonia
NEW GATE
SECOND NORTH WALL?
Church of the Holy Sepulcher
GOLDEN GATE
Dome of the Rock
Upper Aqueduct to Mamilla Pool
Hippicus
Phasael
Patriarch's Pool
FISH GATE?
Mariamme
JAFFA GATE
FIRST NORTH WALL
Western Wall
Citadel
Herod's Palace
WATER GATE?
DUNG GATE
ZION GATE
Virgin's Spring
Lower Aqueduct
Sultan's Pool
Ovens Tower
MEDIEVAL WALL
RAVINE GATE
Siloam Old Pool
FOUNTAIN GATE
EARLY SOUTH WALL
DUNG GATE

The Palestine Exploration Fund opened up a great section of the "Jebusite and Solomonic" walls, overlooking the Kidron above the Gihon Spring ("The Virgin's Foundatin"). A total of 400 feet of east wall, including bastions, towers, glacis, and inner and outer wall, in some places 27 feet wide, came to light. Its course suggests how very small was the capital of the warrior king, who was too busy to build an elegant capital and Temple, as his son and successor Solomon was able to do. The finding of the "great western gate" and wall established the general boundary of David's City and of the south-eastern section of Jerusalem until possibly the Roman era.

Manasseh (c. 687-642 B.C.) is credited by II Chron. 33:14 with building "an outer wall

Jerusalem by night — the west wall near Jaffa Gate

to the city of David, on the west side of Gihon, in the valley, even to the entrance of the fish gate".

Nehemiah's Wall seems to have followed the wall of the early Monarchy on the west, south and east. But at the Hippicus Tower (near the present Jaffa Gate) it moved north-west, forming a new line, containing possibly what was the "Corner Gate". Then it ran north-east, pierced by the Gate of Ephraim, the Old Gate, and the Fish Gate; touched the north-western angle of the Temple Area at the strong Baris which Herod later strengthened to form the castle or fortress Antonia. It was the outermost wall in the time of Christ. The book of Nehemiah describes the Jerusalem walls and gives an account of the craftsmen and artisans who rebuilt them in the 5th century B.C.

Herod surrounded the elegant sanctuary area he developed with beautifully fashioned masonry walls. Portions of these are still seen in the Western ("Wailing") Wall and other stretches, with the giant "cornerstone" (Ps. 118:22); Matt. 21:42) at the southeast angle of the wall, where the masonry rises 75 feet above the present ground level and goes an undetermined distance below it.

41

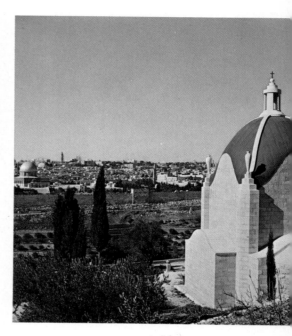

Left:
The Mount of Olives in the east — view from the Temple Area.

Below:
Jerusalem — view from the Mount of Olives. On the right: Dominus Flevit (Luke 19:41)

THE VALLEY OF JEHOSHAPHAT has been identified since the 4th century A.D. as being part of the wide Kidron Valley, extending between the plateau where Jerusalem lies and the Mount of Olives, the scene where all nations must stand before the LORD on the Day of Righteous Judgement (Joel 3:2). The belief of countless thousands in Kidron as the scene of the Last Judgement is attested by the presence of thousands of Jewish and Moslem tombs lining both sides of the Valley. Since pre-Exile times Jews chose to be buried here, that they might be near the place of "the Last Day".

THE SECOND WALL apparently began between the towers of Hippicus and Phasael in Herod's palace near the Jaffa Gate and ran around part of the first Northern wall as far as Antonia at the north-western angle of the Temple Area. Its line was inside the present northern wall.

THE THIRD NORTH WALL was erected by Herod Agrippa I c. A.D.42, to enclose suburban Bezetha and other sections north of the former city wall. It ran at some distance north of the present city wall (that of Hadrian II c. A.D. 135). Almost 800 yards of it have been discovered and studied by the American School of Oriental Research, the (former) Palestine Department of Antiquities, the Jewish Exploration Society and the Hebrew University of Jerusalem.

The present northern wall of Jerusalem appears to be in line with Hadrian's structure of c. 135 A.D. There was no wall on this course earlier than this date. Much of the masonry seen in Jerusalem's picturesque walls and gates today is due to Suleiman the Magnificent (1541-2 A.D.). The observing eye can detect a great variety of types and qualities of masonry, indicating remains from successive buildings and the re-use of materials. The average height of the walls is 38 feet. They enclose an irregular quadrangle c. 2 1/2 miles in circumference.

Jaffa Gate and the Citadel

STARTING POINT — THE CITADEL NEAR THE JAFFA GATE

THE CITADEL is an extensive Medieval fortress, now consisting of several towers connected and enclosed by strong walls, and surrounded by a moat, parts of which are now filled up. If we include the underground parts, it dates from the Hebrew period, down through the Roman and other occupations. The most magnificent feature of the wall of Herod the Great was the three-towered structure which stood near the present Jaffa Gate (see picture and description on page 18). After Herod's death, when Jerusalem came under the Roman Procurators of the sub-province, Herod's palace became their residence while in Jerusalem — Caesarea being the capital. By the Crusaders the Citadel was called the Tower of the Pisans. In its present form it dates chiefly from the early 14th century, and is a good example of the architecture of fortresses of the period. The picturesque minaret at the north-west corner is connected with a mosque from the Moslem period.

THE JAFFA GATE, so named because it opens on the Jaffa Road, is called in Arabic Bab el-Khalil, or Gate of the Friend, since it also opens on the road to Hebron, and the Arabic name for the latter is El Khalil (from the fact that it was the home of Abraham, the "friend" of God). The Jaffa Gate proper is the portal to the north of the large breach through which the road now runs over the old Citadel moat. This part of the moat was purposely filled in and the roadway built, in honour of the visit of ex-Kaiser Wilhelm in 1898; there was theretofore, a low wall across the trench separating the Citadel from the gate tower. Entering, we come into an open Square, on the south of which is the El-Kala'a, or the Citadel, one part of which has for many years been mistakenly called the Tower of David. The square is generally a rendezvous of a diversified and interesting crowd. (A government Tourist Information office is near the gate on the left).

43

Above: West wall leading to Jaffa Gate
Right: The New Gate

STARTING outside the Jaffa Gate, going north, the road runs parallel with the west Wall, turns east at the Allenby Square, skirts the north-western corner of the wall, to go down the hill along a stretch of the northern wall, passing the modern New Gate (Heb. Hasha'ar Hakhadash, Arab. Bal el-Jedid).

At the bottom of the hill we come to the Damascus Gate (Heb. Sha'ar Shechem, Arab. Bab el-Amud). The meaning of the Arabic name is "Gate of the Pillar", which affords an interesting link with the past history of this part of Jerusalem. On the 5th century Medeba Map, the Jerusalem section

Damascus Gate — Northern Wall

shows a colonnaded street, starting at this gate, and running through the city; over this gate is shown a high pillar, which is apparently the origin of the modern Arabic name. Another Arabic name for the gate is Bab en-Nasr, the Gate of Victory; being the most imposing of the portals, it is the one by which conquerors usually entered the city. The name "Damascus" was used because it opens on the road to Damascus. The moat which formerly ran along the base of the wall, both west and east of the gate, has gradually filled up with debris. This is the largest of all the gates; the ornamental battlements, and the outstanding windows and sculptured ornaments give this gate a very imposing effect. The walls on either side are flanked inward from the towers placing the gate itself fruther in than its curtain walls, which naturally makes for its greater strength in time of attack from without. It seems strange that it should stand on such low ground in relation to that just outside it. The passage itself makes two right angles. In the north wall of the first angle, to the left, is seen, a few feet above the roadway, the top of an arch of an earlier gate. This is a good demonstration of the process of filling up, which has taken place through the centuries in old Jerusalem — one stratum of buildings being superimposed on the ruins of the old, while the Past keeps its secrets hidden until the spade of the archaeologist reveals and reads them.

Medeba Map

On the outside of the gate, the stones forming the lower courses are very large, and on the right side, west, have recently (before 1948) been laid bare portions of earlier walls, constructed of large and well-cut stones, several meters below the surface; and subterranean chambers have been found under the towers. Above the gateway, on the outside, an Arabic inscription records that Sultan Suleiman restored the gate in 1537. From here we shall proceed along the top of the wall; but before ascending, we will make a detour to visit the Garden Tomb and other places in the vicinity. This road which starts at Allenby Square as "Hatzanhanim" (Paratroopers) road and runs parallel with the north city wall, continues east as the Suleiman Road.

Returning to the Damascus Gate, we shall ascend the Wall by steps to the left of the Gate, inside, and proceed eastwards on the ramparts to Herod's Gate, noticing Calvary near the Garden Tomb on the way. In the moat below us, on the south side of the trench, a short distance from Damascus Gate, is the entrance to Solomon's Quarries, and opposite it in the same cutting is Jeremiah's Grotto, which may have been a part of the same quarries before this broad

cut in the rock was made, separating the Hill of Calvary from Mt. Bezetha.

JEREMIAH'S GROTTO. Tradition places here the grotto in which the prophet Jeremiah wrote the book of Lamentations, and in which he was buried (?).

SOLOMON'S QUARRIES. The entrance is at the base of the rocky cliff on which the wall of Bezetha stands. It is an underground quarry, which runs southwards for a distance of about 550 feet, measured in a straight line; its breadth is considerably less. The roof is supported by large pillars of rock. Generally it is considered that the tremendous stones for Solomon's Temple were quarried here. The stone is milk-white, and Josephus, in speaking of that Temple, says that it is like a mountain of snow and that it was built entirely of white stone (Josephus Ant, VII.III 2). The Bible account tells us that the stones for the Temple were prepared in the quarry, and that "there was neither hammer nor axe nor any tool of iron heard in the house, while it was in building" (I Kings 7:7).

Ancient gate below Damascus Gate

Entrance to Solomon's Quarries

It was outside this part of the city that Edgar Atheling with his English contingent, was stationed in the siege of Jerusalem in the First Crusade; the Camp of Godfrey De Bouillon stood on the hill near the north-east corner of the city, now occupied by the Rockefeller Archaeological Museum.

Presently we pass over (or near) Herod's Gate (Arab. Bab ez-Zahreh); the name probably comes from the fact that the house of Herod Antipas was shown not far from this gate in the Middle Ages.

Herod's Gate

The rock of Bezetha

The view in many directions from this section of the ramparts is both interesting and beautiful: In the north distance is Mount Scopus, with its groves of pine trees, the magnificent new buildings of the Hebrew University, Hadassah Medical Center and the British Military Cemetery; and intervening south of it is the Kidron Valley. The part of the Kidron lying in the region of Gethsemane, extending in both directions, is sometimes called the Valley of Jehoshaphat (see II Sam. 8:16). In the New Testament Kidron (Kedron) is spelled Cedron (John 18:1).

The north-eastern corner-tower of the Wall is called "Tower of the Storks" (Arab. Burj Laklak). Along here the moat is deeper than in other sections.

After turning the corner we face the tomb-covered slopes of the Mount of Olives on which is the old Jewish Cemetery. Gethsemane is at its base. On the city side we have a good prospect of the Haram, or Temple Area; while just west of us is the depression called the Eastern Gully, in which lies the Pool of Bethesda. Passing behind the Convent of St. Anne, we arrive at St. Stephen's (or The Lions) Gate where we will leave the wall and, going out through the gate, follow the path southwards through the Moslem Cemetery and along the foot of the rampart.

47

The Lions Gate or St. Stephen's Gate

St. Stephen's Gate is called so by Europeans because tradition points out the place of the Protomartyr's stoning near here; by the Jews it is called the Lion's Gate (Sha'ar Ha'arayot), on account of the sculptured lions that adorn its eastern front. The Arabs call it Bab el-Asbat (Gate of the Tribes); Christian Arabs (and others) call it Bab Sitti Miryam — the Gate of Our Lady Mary — since it leads out to the Church of the Virgin, near Gethsemane. The gate is thought to date from Sultan Suleiman, although the lions on its front are those of the later Egyptian Sultan Beibars. In this vicinity stood, in the time of Christ, the Probatic Gate (Sheep Gate), so named from the fact that here used to be brought in the large flocks of sheep for sale to those about to sacrifice in the Temple, and for other purposes. The road inside leads to Via Dolorosa. About 300 feet from the Gate is the massive Herodian Tower, incoporated into the present fortification. Further south is the beautiful facade of the (closed) Golden Gate, with its ornate Byzantine arches.

The Golden Gate (Heb. Sha'ar Ha'rakhamim, Arab. Bab ed-Dahriyeh) is a beautiful structure of two arches, the northern of which is

The Golden Gate — Moslem Cemetery

called Gate of Repentance (Arab. Bab et-Tobeh), and the southern — Gate of Mercy (Arab. Bab er-Rahmeh). In Herod's Temple the gate "Shushan" probably occupied the site of the present Golden Gate. In its present form the gate is at least as old as the 7th century. In 810 it was, with the exception of a small opening, built up and closed. During the Crusader occupation it was opened twice a year, once on Palm Sunday and once on the "Feast of the Raising of the Cross"; on the former, a procession of people and priests, carrying palm branches, came from Olivet and entered the city here.

The interior of the gate is very beautifully ornamented; the low arches are borne on columns and engaged pillars, with beautiful capitals; the frieze too is handsome. The outer side is no less beautiful than the interior.

In this region, outside the ramparts have been found remains of more ancient city walls, now covered; and a short distance to the south next to some huge drafted

**Archaeological excavations
near Western Wall**

blocks, the small built-up Crusader Postern, on whose lintel can be seen a faint, painted cross in a rayed circle, done by the Crusaders over 800 years ago.

The Corner, at which we shortly arrive, built of very large drafted blocks, formed the south-eastern angle of the wall of Herod's city; that is to say, during the lifetime of Christ. Doubling the corner we come to the wonderful and gigantic courses of the Jewish wall, composed of stones each 6 feet thick and extraordinarily long. Small wonder that such a structure should have withstood the ravages of time and siege for so many hundreds of years; here they tower to a height of 75 feet, and their foundations are laid into the rock 80 feet below the surface; making the entire height of this part of the wall 155 feet. When Sir Charles Warren, of the Palestine Exploration Fund made soundings down to the base he found Phoenician mason-marks painted on some of the lower courses, possibly the work of the Phoenician masons sent down by Hiram from Tyre to his friend Solomon. Starting at this angle and running southward, was also found the Great Wall of Ophel of the early Jewish kings, fortified with towers. The ancient Horse Gate (Jer. 21:40; Neh. 3:28) is thought to have stood here. A few yards from the corner is the walled-up "Single Gate" of the Crusaders, which before being blocked up was an entrance to the so-called Solomon's Stables, where the Knights Templars stabled their animals. A

little further west is the Triple Gate or the Eastern Huldah Gate. About 150 feet away is the angle made by the abutment of the city rampart upon the Temple wall and at this point is seen the eastern portal of still another gate in this vicinity, the Western Huldah Gate or the "Double Gate".

Large scale archaeological excavations near the Western and Southern Walls were started in 1968 on behalf of the Israel Exploration Society and the Institute of Archaeology of the Hebrew University, with the cooperation of the Israel Academy of Humanities and Sciences and the National Parks Authority (detailed reports by Prof. B. Mazar, Director of the excavations and archaeologists who assisted were published by the Israel Exploration Society).

Leaving the site of the archaeological excavations we shall now retrace our steps and descend into the Kidron Valley to the Tomb or Pillar of Absalom, as it is commonly called. Although mentioned in the 4th century, it was not until the 16th that it was regarded as a monument of Absalom, suggested by the passage in II Sam. 18:18, that Absalom, having no son, reared a monument in the "King's Dale" to perpetuate his name. Behind the monument there is a series of rock-hewn chambers known as the Tomb of Jehoshaphat and a short distance to the south is the Grotto of St. James — an extensive series of tomb-chambers cut in the solid rock, probably also Graeco-Roman, in which a 6th century tradition relates that St. James lay concealed without nourishment from the time of Christ's arrest to His resurrection.

From the vestibule a passageway leads to the Tomb of Zachariah, a solid, cubic, rock-hewn monument 29.5 feet high, surmounted by a pyramid. A little farther down the valley, at the entrance to the village, is another rock-cut monument called the Tomb of Pharaoh's Daugher, which belongs to a pre-Exile period. Just beyond this, built on the slope of the Hill of Offence — where Solomon built temples to heathen gods — is the village of Siloam (Arab. Silwan).

The spring of Gihon (Virgin's Fountain, Arab. Ain Sitti Maryam) is situated in a cave

Absalom's Monument and the tombs of Zachariah and St. James in the Kidron Valley

in the wetern wall of the valley, about 350 yards south of the south-eastern angle of the Temple Area. There is a very interesting group of subterranean ducts and channels connected with this fountain. The oldest of these is the famous Dragon Shaft, revealed by the exploration of P.E.F. The second, and perhaps the most interesting channel is the celebrated Siloam Tunnel made by King Hezekiah in the 8th century B.C. It was made at the time of Sennacherib's invasion and in it was found the famous Siloam Inscription. The tunnel connects the spring with the Pool of Siloam, which lies on the other south-west side of Ophel, and in its course, instead of being in a straight line, describes roughly the figure "s", making the length of the tunnel 1750 feet. Its average height, which varies considerably, is about 5 feet and the average width 2½ feet. In the side of the wall was found in 1880, the oldest extant Hebrew inscription, now at Constantinople, which gives a short description of the tunnel, and relates that the cutting was done simultaneously from both ends, the two working parties meeting in the middle.

The Valley Gate of ancient Jerusalem stood near here. Following the valley, southward, the road comes to the junction of the Kidron with the Tyropeon, near which a path leads to the Pool of Siloam. A little further down the valley, near its junction with the Valley of Hinnom the road comes to Job's Well (Arab. Bir Ayoub), which most probably is En Rogel of the Old Testament

(see 2 Sam. 17:17; 1 Kings 1:9). We shall now take a view of the rocky Valley of Hinnom, which bounds Jerusalem on the south and west. Here was built an altar to Moloch, whose abominations and human sacrifices continued to be practiced during many reigns. This high-place was called Tophet, and here the infants were caused "to pass through the fire". King Joash defiled this heathen altar (2 Kings 23:10). Here also, perhaps on the site of Tophet, burned the furnace Gehenna, where the refuse of the city was consumed. The New Testament name for the valley is Gehenna, which is also the Greek word for hell.

The Hill of Evil Counsel (Arab. Ras Abu Tor) is where, according to tradition, Caiaphas possessed a country house. On the slope of the hill is a Greek convent, adjacent to which are several cemeteries, one of which is called Aceldama, or "Field of Blood" (Matt. 27:3-10).

Pool of Siloam

The southern wall before the archaeological excavations

Hezekiah's Tunnel

Archaeological Excavations near Southern Wall

Excavated area near upper southern wall — rebuilt Jewish Quarter seen behind the wall

Archaeological Excavations — Corner of Western and Southern Wall

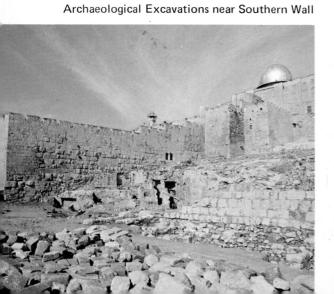

The Dung Gate

Returning to the Pool of Siloam, we shall follow the road up to the Dung Gate of the city in the south (Heb. Sha'ar Ha'ashpot, Arab. Bab el-Magharibeh). The newly built road leading west, along the southern wall, comes soon to Zion Gate (Heb. Sha'ar Zion, Arab. Bab en-Nebi Dahoud, Gate of the Prophet David), which bears an inscription of Suleiman stating that the gate was built in 1541. Close to this gate, on Mt. Zion, are the Church of the Dormition, King David's Tomb and the Upper Room (of the Last Supper) (see pages 24-25).

Zion Gate

In the valley, to the south-west lies the large pool of Birket Es-Sultan. The name refers to the builder of the walls of the city, who restored it in the 16th century. It may, however be the site of a reservoir of the early Jewish period; it is about 500 feet long by about 220 feet wide.

Situated a few hundred yards south of the Jesuit College and close to the King David Hotel is the Herodian sepulchre called the Tomb of Mariamne. It consists of an interesting series of connected chambers cut in the rock, lined with finely cut blocks of white stone. An important feature is the Rolling Stone, for closing the entrance; this is a circular slab about 4 feet in diameter, and one foot deep, which rolls in to close the doorway, similarly to that which sealed the tomb of Christ.

We now approach the picturesque so-called Tower of David or the Citadel of Zion, with its massive towers, its picturesque glacis and slender minaret, to arrive back at the Jaffa Gate.

Jerusalem — view from the Mt. Olives

Snow in Jerusalem —

Orthodox Jew with children on way to
Western Wall

"Hassidim" — pious Jews

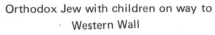

The Citadel and city's west wall at night

And it shall come to pass in the last days, that the mountain of the Lord's house shall be established in the top of the mountains and shall be exalted above the hills; and all nations shall flow unto it...

...And he shall judge among the nations, and shall rebuke many people; and they shall beat their swords into plowshares, and their spears into pruning hooks; nation shall not lift up sword against nation, neither shall they learn war any more.

Isaiah 2:2,4

REUBEN   SIMEON   LEVI

THE TWELVE TRIBES OF ISRAEL

ISRAEL — the name given Jacob by an angel at the Jabbok ford on the eve of his reunion with his brother (Gen. 32:28); and also by God at Bethel (Gen. 35:10). The Genesis account of the activities of Jacob and his sons make the Patriarch the direct ancestor of the Hebrew nation; and his 12 sons the progenitors and heads of the Twelve Tribes of Israel.

BENJAMIN

JOSEPH

JUDAH

ZEBULUN

The Twelve Sons of Israel (Jacob) Who Became Heads of the Twelve Tribes:

Son	Mother	Scripture	Son	Mother	Scripture
Reuben	Leah	Gen. 29:32	Gad	Zilpah[2]	Gen. 30:11
Simeon	Leah	Gen. 29:33	Asher	Zilpah	Gen. 30:13
Levi	Leah	Gen. 29:34	Issachar	Leah	Gen. 30:18
Judah	Leah	Gen. 29:35	Zebulun	Leah	Gen. 30:20
Dan	Bilhah[1]	Gen. 30:5,6	Joseph	Rachel	Gen. 30:24
Naptahli	Bilhah	Gen. 30:8	(later Ephraim		
1: Rachel's maid.			and Manasseh)		
2: Leah's maid.			Benjamin	Rachel	Gen. 35:18

CONQUEST AND INHERITANCE OF THE PROMISED LAND — CANAAN

During and following the conquest the Tribes of Reuben and Gad, together with the half Tribe of Manasseh, received from Moses territory East of the Jordan (Josh. 12:6, 17:5). The other 9½ tribes received their shares when lots were drawn by Eleazar the priest and Joshua at Shiloh (Josh. 14:1,2). The influential Joseph Tribe was represented in the allotment by the two half Tribes of his sons, Ephraim and Manasseh. The priestly house of Levi acquired cities and land by gifts from the other Tribes (Josh. 21). The boundaries of the assignments were fluid (Josh. 13:19). Dan, possibly pushed out by the Philistines, moved from his original territory on poor land in the Northern Shephelah to fertile acreage near the headwaters of the Jordan. The Joseph Tribes and Benjamin held the region of the central highlands, which became the nucleus of the Kingdom of Israel established when the Hebrew Monarchy was divided in about 922 B.C.

NAPHTALI

ISSACHAR

ASHER   GAD   DAN

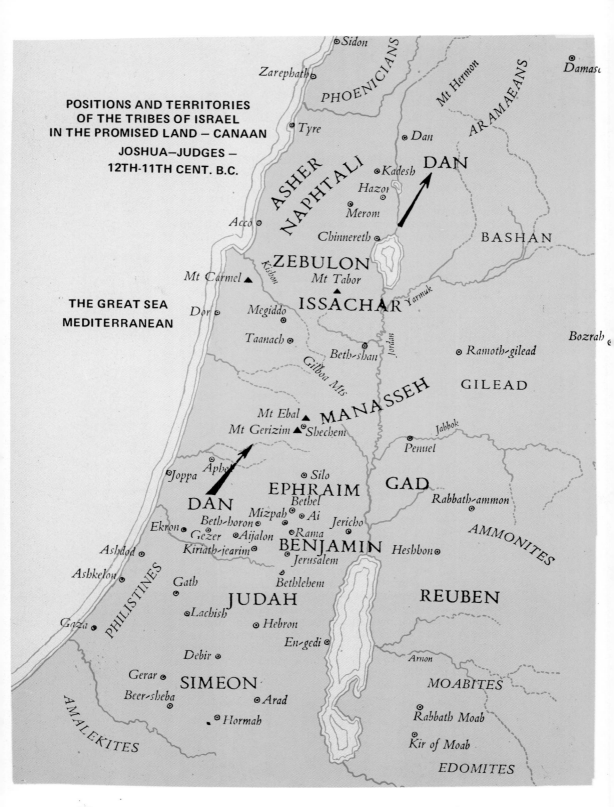

POSITIONS AND TERRITORIES
OF THE TRIBES OF ISRAEL
IN THE PROMISED LAND — CANAAN
JOSHUA—JUDGES —
12TH-11TH CENT. B.C.

PHOENICIANS

ARAMAEANS

Sidon

Zarephath

Mt Hermon

Damascus

ASHER

NAPHTALI

Tyre

Dan

DAN

Kadesh

Hazor

Merom

BASHAN

Acco

Chinnereth

ZEBULON

THE GREAT SEA
MEDITERRANEAN

Mt Carmel ▲

Kishon

Mt Tabor

ISSACHAR

Yarmuk

Dor

Megiddo

Taanach

Beth-shan

Jordan

Ramoth-gilead

Bozrah

Gilboa Mts

GILEAD

MANASSEH

Mt Ebal ▲

Mt Gerizim ▲ *Shechem*

Jabbok

Penuel

Joppa

Aphek

Silo

EPHRAIM

GAD

Bethel

DAN

Mizpah

Ai

Rabbath-ammon

Beth-horon

Jericho

AMMONITES

Ekron

Gezer

Aijalon

Rama

Kiriath-jearim

BENJAMIN

Heshbon

Ashdod

Jerusalem

Ashkelon

Gath

Bethlehem

REUBEN

Gaza

PHILISTINES

JUDAH

Lachish

Hebron

En-gedi

Arnon

Debir

Gerar

SIMEON

Arad

MOABITES

Beer-sheba

Hormah

Rabbath Moab

AMALEKITES

Kir of Moab

EDOMITES

THE CHAGALL WINDOWS AT THE
HADASSAH MEDICAL CENTER IN JERUSALEM

The magnificent, world famous stained-glass windows symbolizing the Twelve Tribes of Israel, designed by Marc Chagall, were installed in the synagogue of the new Hadassah-Hebrew University Medical Center in the Judean hills west of Jerusalem in 1962. They were commissioned by Hadassah, The Women's Zionist Organization of America. Executed in brilliant reds, blues, yellows and greens, the windows for the synagogue, created by the noted French Jewish artist symbolize the twelve sons of Jacob, heads of the tribes, and the blessing by Moses as in Genesis 49 and Deuteronomy 33. The windows are approximately eleven feet high and eight feet wide, and are arranged in groups of three on four sides of the lantern:

	REUBEN	SIMEON	LEVI	
BENJAMIN				JUDAH
JOSEPH				ZEBULUN
NAPHTALI				ISSACHAR
	ASHER	GAD	DAN	

THE BLESSING OF JACOB—ISRAEL

The Blessing of Jacob (Gen. 49:2-27) is one of the most important poems in the Torah (The first five "Books of Moses" — the Pentateuch). It describes prophetically the fortunes and woes of the Twelve Tribes of Israel and their traits in the period of the Judges when each Tribe was fighting its own battles. It is unique in its puns on the names of the Tribes, and its comparison of six of the Tribes to animals and a tree — Judah "a lion's whelp" (v. 9); Issachar "a strong ass" (v. 14); Dan "a serpent" (v. 17); Napthali "a hind let loose" (v. 21); Benjamin "a wolf" (49:27); and Joseph "a fruitful bough" (v. 22).

AND JACOB called unto his sons, and said, Gather yourselves together, that I may tell you that which shall befall you in the last days. Gather yourselves together, and hear, ye sons of Jacob; and hearken unto Israel your father...(Gen. 49:1, 2). AND THIS IS the blessing, wherewith Moses the man of God blessed the children of Israel before his death... (Deut. 33:1).

...for mine house shall be called a house of prayer for all people. — Isaiah 56:7

For I will restore health unto thee, and I will heal thee of thy wounds, saith the LORD; — Jeremiah 30:17

The synagogue at the Hadassah Medical Center Interior — partial view of the Chagall Windows — from left to right: Simeon, Levi, Judah and Zebulon

REUBEN, eldest son of Jacob and Leah, whose window opens the cycle, is blessed first: *Thou art my first born, my might, and the beginning of my strength, the excellency of dignity, and the excellency of power; unstable as water...* (dominant colour is blue — "water"...) In the blessing of Jacob Rueben's instability is ruefully pondered by the dying Patriarch. But his nobler side is vividly brought out in the Joseph* story, for it was Reuben who advised against killing Joseph and suggested instead the casting of the youth into a pit, from which he planned to extricate him later and restore him to their father (Gen. 37:22,29).

SIMEON, the second son of Jacob and Leah is next: *...Simeon and Levi are brethern; weapons of violence their kinship. Let not my soul come into their council...for in their anger they slew men, and in their selfwill they houghed oxen. Cursed be their anger...* (dominant colour is also blue). He was not one of the major figures in Israel's history, and his destiny is linked with that of his brother Judah, with whose territory and interest those of Simeon seemed to blend. Along with his full brothers Reuben, Levi, and Judah, Simeon was a leader in avenging the rape of their sister Dina by Shechem (Gen. 34).

LEVI, the third son of Jacob and Leah: *...They shall teach Jacob thy Judgements, and Israel thy law; they shall put incense before thee, and whole burnt sacrifice upon thine altar* (Deut. 33:10) (the colour is yellow, solar exaltation and divine light). Levi died in Egypt at an advanced age (Ex. 6:16). Miriam, Aaron, and Moses were his great-grandchildren, through Kohath's line. Levi was singled out among the sons of Jacob: among the sons of Levi (Num. 3:14-39) the high priest Aaron and his line (3:1-4) marked the exact center of the concentric circles, the climax of Israel's racial history. Rabbinic and Hellenistic literature enhanced the stature of Levi, regarding him as visited by God's special favour because he represented, in a sense, the priesthood.

61

JUDAH, the 4th son of Jacob and Leah: *He washed his garments in wine, And his vesture in the blood of grapes...Judah is a Lion's whelp... the sceptre shall not depart from Judah...* This Tribe was, along with that of Ephraim* the most important in the history of the Hebrew people. From the Tribe of Judah came the line of Boaz, Jesse, and David. During the Exodus Judah and his Tribe encamped with Zebulun and Issachar on the eastern side of the sanctuary (Num. 2:3). The men of Judah supported Saul; annointed his successor, David, at Hebron (2 Sam. 2:4); and supported him and his heirs at Jerusalem (1 Kings 12:20) (colour of window — red).

ZEBULUN, 6th son of Leah and Jacob, and the 10th of Jacob (Gen. 30:20): *Zebulun shall dwell at the shore of the sea, And he shall be a shore for ships, And his flank be upon Sidon...* (window: blue against the dominant red background). The Tribe of Zebulun held territory as being "at the haven of the sea" (Gen. 49:13), with easy access to harbours. Though actually cut off from the Mediterranean by Asher, and from the Sea of Galilee by Naphtali and Issachar, Zebulunites were in convenient reach of rich markets like Sidon. Their terrirtory, though not large, was fertile, including a small portion of the Plain of Jezreel-Esdraelon.

ISSACHAR, Jacob's 9th son, his fifth by Leah (Gen. 30:14-18): *...Issachar is a large boned ass, couching down between the sheepfolds, For he saw a resting-place that was good, And the land that it was pleasant, And he bowed his shoulders to bear, and became a servant under taskwork...* (the window is green). The Plain of Jezreel-Esdraelon was within Issachar's lot. The "Via Maris" ("Way of the Sea") passed through Issachar, and was a source of easy revenue to those who lived there. Deborah and Barak were probably of Issachar (Judg. 5:15). The blessing on Issachar voiced by Moses was for the sacrifices which the Tribe maintained on mountain high places patronized by the neighbouring Phoenicians, who possessed "the abundance of the seas" and "treasures of the sands" (Deut. 33:18).

DAN, son of Jacob and Bilhah, handmaid of Rachel (Gen. 30:5): *...Dan shall judge his people, as one of the Tribes of Israel. Dan shall be a serpent in the way, an adder in the path, That biteth the horse's heels, so that his rider falleth backward...* (dominant colour of the window is blue). After the period of the Judges the Danites, having failed either to conquer or to assimilate their predecessors, and feeling the pressure of the Philistines, sought territory farther north (Judg. 18:1-31). Finding in the town of Laish, at the foot of Mt. Hermon near the headwaters of the Jordan, the pleasant and secure spot they sought, a group of Danites seized control of the domestic priest and local gods, smote the citizens, burned the city and renamed it "Dan" (Judg. 18:31).

GAD, eldest son of Zilpah and Jacob (Gen. 30:11, 35:26): *...Gad, a troop shall troop upon him; But he shall troop upon their heel...* (window: green). Gad's territory granted by Moses (Num. 32; Deut. 16:20), lay northeast of the Dead Sea, bounded on the west by the Jordan, on the east, by the territory of Ammon, on the north, by the Heshbon gorge, and on the south by the gorge of Jabbok. Gadites, together with other eastern Tribes, supported David against Saul, and after Solomon's death supported the revolt of Jeroboam, allowing him to make his capital at Penuel (1 Kings 12:25). The Tribe was deported by Tiglath-pileser III in 734 B.C.

ASHER, son of Jacob and Zilpah, Leah's hand-maid: *...As for Asher, his bread shall be fat, And he shall yield royal dainties...* And in Moses' blessing: *...He shall bathe his foot in oil...* (colour of window: green): Asher became the head of a Hebrew Tribe assigned to a strip of coast along the Mediterranean, reaching from Mt. Carmel to Phoenicia, a fertile territory supplying food to royal tables, but never wholly subdued by Asher, for it included such powerful cities as Accho (Akko-Acre), Tyre and Sidon (Judg. 1:31).

NAPHTALI, the second son of Bilhah, handmaid of Rachel, and Jacob: *...Naphtali is a hind let loose; He giveth goodly word...* (like the window of Levi, the dominant colour of the window is yellow): Naphtali from the Hebrew "naphtulim", "wrestlings", because Rachel had wrestled with Leah and won, by the birth of a son to her handmaid, or had "wrestled" with God in petition for a child. The adventurous, free young spirit of the men of Naphtali led to their being likened in the blessing of Jacob to "a hind let loose" (Gen. 49: 21). The territory which fell to Naphtali's lot as a member of the northernmost tribal group was all north of the Plain of Jezreel-Esdraelon, and was cut off from the southern tribes by a chain of Canaanite fortresses. It was excellent land along the west and northwest shores of the Sea of Galilee and the Upper Jordan.

JOSEPH, the son of Jacob and Rachel. The account of his birth is given in Gen. 30:22-24: *...Joseph is a fruitful vine, A fruitful vine by a fountain, its branches run over a wall (he shall be widely blessed...with blessings of heaven above...* (window in radiant yellow): Joseph's dreams incurred his brothers' jealousy; he was sold into slavery; became Potiphar's steward; resisted temptation; interpreted the dreams of Pharaoh himself; was made a ruler in Egypt and married; prepared for famine; received his hungry brothers and father, who settled in Goshen, Egypt. The name "Joseph" is used to denote the combined tribes of Ephraim and Manasseh (Josh. 17:14); the Northern Kingdom (1 Kings 11:38); and the Israelite people as a whole (Ps. 80). It is possible that part of his tribe made early settlement in Canaan before the Exodus.

BENJAMIN, the 12th and last son of Jacob and Rachel, renamed so after his dying mother had called him "Ben-oni" ("son of my sorrow"): *...Benjamin is a wolf that raveth; In the morning he devoureth the prey and at evening he divideth the spoil...* (predominantly blue window): Full brother of Joseph whose birth took place in Canaan (on the outskirts of Bethlehem). The boundaries of the Tribe of Benjamin in general were: the Jordan on the east; a line from Jericho to Bethel on the north; a line from Beth-horon to Kirjath-jearim on the west; and on the south by a line from Beth-horon to the Dead Sea. The boundary between Benjamin and Judah seems to have run through the city of Jerusalem (Judg. 1:8, 1:21), with the Temple in Benjamin and its arcaded courts in Judah.

The synagogue at the Hadassah Medical Center (exterior)

The Hadassah-Hebrew University Medical Center

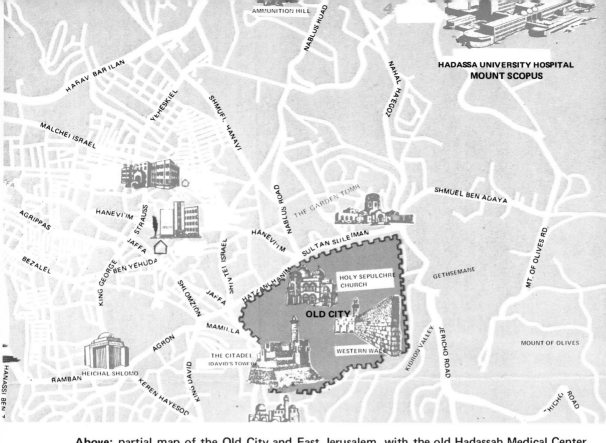

Above: partial map of the Old City and East Jerusalem, with the old Hadassah Medical Center on Mount Scopus

Below: partial map of the New City of Jerusalem, with the New Hadassah-Hebrew University Medical Center near Ein Karem, about 5 miles west of the city

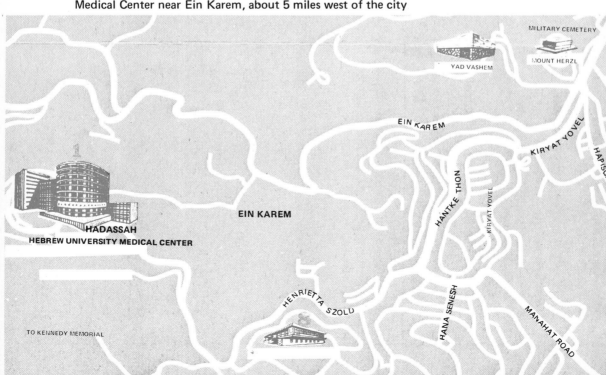

VISITS TO NATIONAL AND PUBLIC INSTITUTIONS
AND TO SITES IN WESTERN JERUSALEM

Herzl Avenue, leading west, begins at the northern end of Jaffa Road near "Egged's" main bus terminal, close to "Binyanei-Ha'uma" Convention Center and Auditorium. Opposite, from the main Tel-Aviv highway which leads north, a road goes via Sanhedria and Ramat-Eshcol, passes by "Ammunition Hill" and leads to **Mount Scopus** in the east.

Passing **"Kiryat-Moshe"** quarter (named after Sir Moses Montefiore) Herzl Avenue reaches the pleasantly situated garden residential area (former suburb) of **Beth-Hakerem** ("House of Vineyard"), in which are the Hebrew Teachers Seminary and the **WIZO** (Women's International Zionist Organization) **Babies Home.**

The Military Cemetery, on the slope of the hill to the right, is the resting place for Jerusalemites who fell in all of Israel's wars: War of Liberation (1948), Sinai Campaign (1956), the Six Day War (1967), and the Yom Kippur War (1973). Buried here are also fallen members of the Underground Organizations, Volunteers in the British Army (2nd World War) and others.

Mount Herzl, the National Shrine, is the resting place of the founder of the Zionist Movement whose remains were brought here from Vienna after the establishment of the State of Israel. From Herzl's Tomb on the summit, a beautiful panoramic view of Jerusalem is obtained, and a short distance from here is the resting place of Israel's National Leaders.

Yad Vashem Memorial (Mt. Memorial) is on a neighbouring summit close to Mt. Herzl. The name **Yad Vashem** ("Monument and Name") was given to this National Memorial for the six million Jews who were killed by the Nazis during World War II from Isaiah's prophecy (Isa. 56:5): **"Even unto them will I give in mine house and within my walls a place and a name... I will give them an everlasting name, that shall not be cut off".**

Ein Karem. A road descends from Mt. Herzl to the picturesque village in the hills, which, since early days has been identified with the **"city in the hill country of Judea"**, where, according to Luke 1, Mary visited the cousin Elisabeth and where St. John the Baptist was born. Entering the village, a lane to the right leads to the large Franciscan **Monastery of St. John**. The present church dates from the late 17th century. Seven steps in the left apse lead down to the Birth Grotto of the Baptist. The heart of the village, the spring to which it owes its name "Ein Karem — spring of Vineyard", has been associated since Crusader days with Mary's visit.

On the left is the small convent of the **Nuns of the Rosary**, and nearby is the Russian Nuns Orthodox church. Pilgrim tradition has it, that the wealthy priest Zacharias had two houses in Ein Karem: A town house, where St. John was born, and a country house, where Mary visited Elisabeth. The present church stands on the ruins of a Crusader church. The **Visitation Church** is a work of Barluzzi, the highly gifted architect who built many churches all over the country.

Bayit-Vegan is the name of the residential suburb near Mt. Herzl. Continuing west via **Kiryat-Yovel** and other newly built suburbs, the road comes to a junction, from where, one road to the left ascends the hill known as Giv'at Orah and leads to the impressive momument of the **John F. Kennedy Memorial**. Another road, overlooking Ein Karem in the valley, leads down and arrives at the new **Hadassah-Hebrew University** Medical **Center**.

Hadassah, the Women's Zionist Organization of America was founded in 1912 by Miss Henrietta Szold, American-Jewish scholar, writer and pioneer Zionist. Numbering today over 340.000 members, the internationally-known Hadassah Medical Organization is based, since 1961, in the **Hadassah-Hebrew University Medical Center** at Ein Karem, Jerusalem, to which are being added, rebuilt and expanded facilities on **Mount Scopus**, Hadassah's first "hill of healing". **The old Hadassah Medical Center** near the original Hebrew University campus on Mount Scopus, consisting of the Hospital, School of Nursing and the Medical School, was cut off from the city of Jerusalem for about 19 years, until the Six Day War in 1967. The New Medical Center includes: the Rothschild-Hadassah-University Hospital, Outpatient Clinics, School of Nursing, Hebrew University Medical School, Mother and Child Pavilion, School of Dentistry founded by Alpha Omega, John F. Kennedy reception and information center, headquarters for Ya'al volunteers, the synagogue crowned by stained glass windows of the famed artist Marc Chagall, Administration Building.

Hills of Judea — Wilderness of St. John

Ein Karem — The Franciscan Monastery of St. John

The Wilderness of St. John may be reached by a road leading north-west from the Convent des Dames de Zion in Ein Karem. Through olive groves the road arrives at the bottom of the valley, from where, a three mile long track comes to the "Wilderness".

Mount Herzl — Guards of honour near Herzl's Tomb

70

GULF OF MEXICO

New Orleans•

Mississippi

NORTH

AMERICA

GREAT LAKES

CANADIAN SHIELD

SIGSBEE KNOLLS
•-1342

MISSISSIPPI CONE

-9984

CONTINENTAL SHELF

-120

COASTAL PLAIN

APPALACHIAN MOUNTAINS

•Mt. Mitchell
6684

St. Lawrence

Havana•

CUBA

Miami•

-200.

BAHAMA ISLANDS

BLAKE PLATEAU
3900
(2100)

-24

Washington•

New York•

Boston•

-12.

-228.

SABLE ISLAND

CAPE BRETON ISLAND

MIQUELON ISLANDS

-42.

GRAND BANKS

GREATER ANTILLES

PUERTO RICO TRENCH
-27,500;
Atlantic Ocean's
deepest point

10,417
(26417)

OUTER RIDGE

-18,150

HATTERAS ABYSSAL PLAIN

-17,400

HUDSON CANYON

-5412.

KELVIN SEAMOUNT
(10,588)

-4590.

-330

ISLAND OF NEWFOUNDLAND

NARES

-19,200.

ABYSSAL PLAIN

BERMUDA RISE

BERMUDA ISLANDS

259.

-16,200.

SOHM ABYSSAL PLAIN

LAURENTIAN CONE

-168. FLEMISH CAP

-15,420.

LESSER ANTILLES

-9342.

-18,300

-17,400.

CORNER SEAMOUNTS

-15,900.

-336 MILNE SEAMOUNT (15,664)

-14,760

10,417
(26417)

MID-ATLANTIC

-13,200.

-6978
(9022)

-12,844.
(9022)

-12,000

OCEANOGRAPHER FRAC-
TURE

-15,300.

ATLANTIC OCEAN FLOOR

•-12000 Depth in feet below sea level   •9000 Height above sea level
(14000) Height above the 16,000-foot average depth of the abyssal plains

Produced in the Geographic Art Division

National Geographic Society

MELVIN M. PAYNE, PRESIDENT

for THE NATIONAL GEOGRAPHIC MAGAZINE

MELVILLE BELL GROSVENOR, EDITOR-IN-CHIEF; FREDERICK G. VOSBURGH, EDITOR

WILLIAM N. PALMSTROM, CHIEF, GEOGRAPHIC ART DIVISION

Based on bathymetric studies by Bruce C. Heezen and Marie Tharp of the Lamont Geological Observatory

Painted by Heinrich C. Berann, Compiled by Leo J. Boberschmidt

HORIZONTAL SCALE 1: 30, 412, 800 OR 480 MILES TO THE INCH AT THE EQUATOR
VERTICAL SCALE EXAGGERATED

Mercator Projection
JUNE, 1968

HUDSON BAY

•-768
•-330
•-18

•-462
(15538)
•-10500

MID-OCEAN CANY

CONTINENTAL SLOPE

•-5580

•Godthåb

GREENLAND

•-7800

The Jerusalem Military Cemetery

71

The Yad Vashem Memorial — "Ohel Yizkor" — Hall of Remembrance
The Walls are built of large unhewn black lava rocks. On the mosaic floor are inscribed the
names of the 21 largest concentration camps and near the wall in the west burns a light.

The Shrine of the Book

The Menorah near the Knesset Bldg.

Shrine of the Book (Interior)

THE NEW CITY OF JERUSALEM

Today's Jerusalem, the Capital of the state of Israel, as afore said, is quite different from the historical Holy City; the new, modern "West Jerusalem" as it is called, is about 135 years old only, and until 1948 was a western suburb, or a group of western suburbs of the historic Jerusalem, the Old City within the walls. Despite the fact that all public buildings and institutions were and are situated in the new city, the whole orientation was conditioned by the existence of the old city. Only after the withdrawal of Ibrahim Pasha, the Egyptian, in 1840, and with the improvement of securi-

ty, the citizens of Jerusalem started to leave the safe but overpopulated walled city and to build permanent buildings in the open country.

The history of New Jerusalem begins with the construction of two Windmills which still stand and exist, but their claim as historical buildings has never been deservedly recognized. Sir Moses Montefiore built Yemin-Moshe in 1858, the oldest Jewish 'suburb' outside the walls. The enormous Russian Compound was constructed after the Crimean War, on what used to be Jerusalem's "main square", horsemarket and parade grounds of the garrison. Various quarters for Jewish immigrants came soon into being, Catholic monasteries were built and the intervening space filled with houses. This development, however, was slow until it gained impetus with the British Mandate. New Jerusalem, as it stands now, was built by homecoming Jews, and with the money the homecoming Jews brought to the country.

From 1948, after heavy fighting and long siege, to 1967, Jerusalem was a divided city, with the front-line — later the Cease-fire line — stretching from the Sanhedria Quarter in the north, to the hill of Ramat-Rachel overlooking Bethlehem in the south. Desperately contested was the sector where, near the old city walls, the Israeli and Jordanian positions were less than fifty yards apart.

New Jerusalem

The "Mandelbaum Gate" which was the only crossing-point and transit between the two halves of cruelly divided Jerusalem from 1948 to 1967, was no "gate" at all, but just the roadblock with customs barracks, divided by an open space of No-Man's land. This "gate" (Mandelbaum = Almonds tree), by the way, does not owe its poetic name to an idyllic orchard of almond trees, but to an unfortunate Mr. Mandelbaum, in whose half-destroyed estate the Mixed Armistice Commision of the U.N. resided.

New Jerusalem's shopping centers are Jaffa Road and Ben-Yehuda Street, which join at Zion Square and are connected by King George Avenue, with the residential quarters to the west, north and south.

The planning of Jerusalem from 1948 to 1967 had to accept the fact that any development eastwards was not possible. The obvious solution was development of the west. Many new quarters, residential and industrial, as well as many National Institutions have been built: The "Knesset" (Par-

Yad Vashem Memorial

liament), President's House, Government offices, the new campus of the Hebrew University, the Israel Museum and the Shrine of the book, Mt. Herzl, the Military Cemetery, Yad Vashem Memorial, the new Hadassah Medical Center, the Kennedy Memorial Binyanei-Ha'ouma Auditorium and Convention Center, the Jerusalem Theatre, and more. New cultural centers, hotels, restaurants and places of entertainment have been erected and established, and since 1967, when the city was united, building, development and construction has reached areas on all sides and parts, formerly near or across the old border. The population of west, modern Jerusalem grew from about 84.000 in 1948 to about 284,000 in 1979, and the total population of the united city, where Jews, Christians and Moslems live peacefully together, numbers now 384,000 (May 1979).

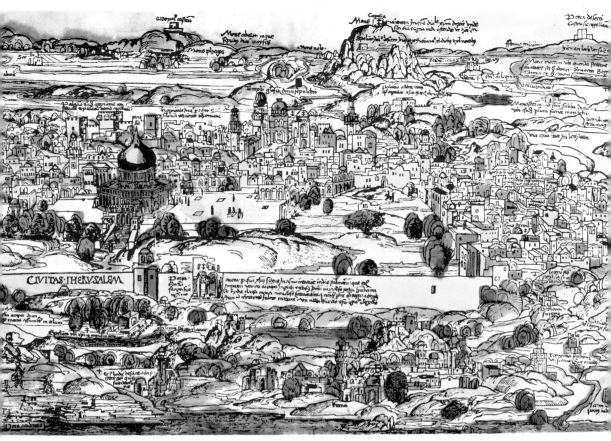

Jerusalem, a drawing, London, 1577

TO BE IN JERUSALEM

To conclude a fair summary of what it means to be in Jerusalem, which is "builded as a city that is compact together" (Psalms 122:2—3):—

... History records no other hallowed site, the uninterrupted veneration of which is older than that of Jerusalem. True, the temples of Karnak, the Zikkurath of Sumer were old, when Melchizedek, King of Salem, brought forth bread and wine for Abraham — "and he was the priest of the most high God". But these shrines are empty ruins, broken shells of a faith forgotten for thousands of years, whilst the prayers of Jerusalem have not ceased for thousands of years. The longing for Jerusalem has remained irradicable in the heart of mankind; Neither Babylonian nor Roman destruction or other conquests could change the deep-rooted identification of the earthly with the heavenly Jerusalem.

This blend of old and new, composed of people of the most varied backgrounds, this city has an atmosphere that defies definintion, as does the landscape of Jerusalem, which is the symbol of her soul. — The skyline of Mount Scopus, with the Hebrew University, leading to the Mount of Olives, where the Ascension Tower points to heaven; the view of the blue mountains of Moab in the east, and that other over the Plain of Rephaim to the hills in the west, set with walls, domes and towers; they are always present, and they never let you forget, what it means to be in Jerusalem.

NEW CITY OF JERUSALEM (partial map-city center)

Detail from AMIR's Pictorial map — 1976

FROM JERUSALEM — SOUTH AND EAST

*   **To Bethlehem, Hebron & Beer-Sheva**

**To Bethany, Jericho, Qumran, Dead Sea,
En-Gedi, Masada, Sodom & the Negev**

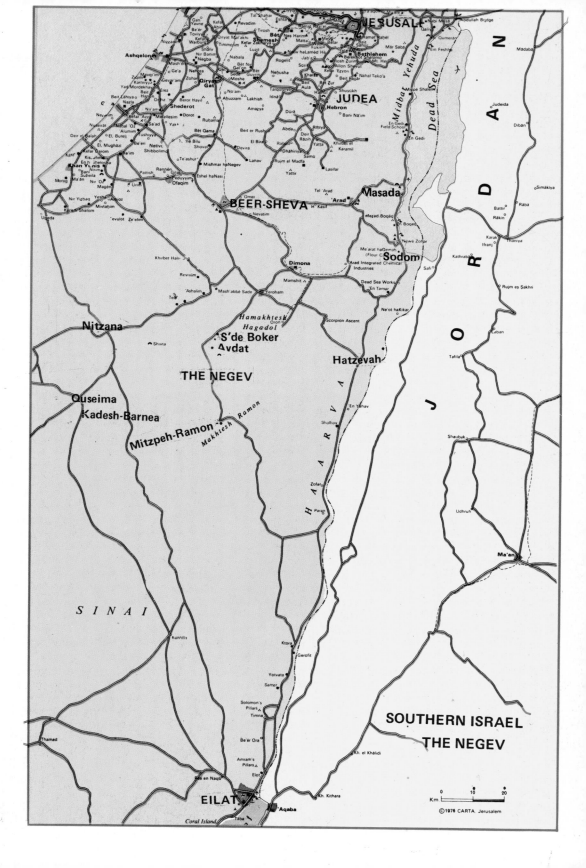

JERUSALEM

Ashqelon

Qiryat Gat

Shederot

BEER-SHEVA

Khan Yunis

Hebron

JUDEA

Masada

Sodom

Dimona

Nitzana

Hamakhtesh Hagadol

S'de Boker

Avdat

Hatzevah

THE NEGEV

Quseima
Kadesh-Barnea

Mitzpeh-Ramon

Makhtesh Ramon

Midbar Yehuda

Dead Sea

J O R D A N

Ma'an

S I N A I

H A R A R A V A

EILAT

Aqaba
Coral Island

SOUTHERN ISRAEL

THE NEGEV

Km 0   10   20

©1976 CARTA, Jerusalem

FROM JERUSALEM TO BETHLEHEM

The road leads south through the Valley of Rephaim, or Valley of Giants, a frequent camping-ground of the Philistines, and the scene of two defeats inflicted on them by David (2 Sam. 5:18—20). Further on, about half way to Bethlehem, we pass on the left side of the road the "Well of the Magi" which, tradition has it as resting place of the "wise men", who, losing sight of the star, saw the reflection of it in the water. By the Arabs it is said to have been the resting place of Mary on her way to Bethlehem.

On the hill ahead is the large Greek Monastery of Mar Elyas (St. Elijah) which occupies a commanding position and the roof of which affords a fine view of the blue mountains of Moab and the Dead Sea in the east; Bethlehem and Beth-Jala surrounded by olive trees on the south and, looking back, the beautiful panorama of the new city of Jerusalem in the north-west. The Franks found the place destroyed and rebuilt it, in 1160. The legend connecting the place with the flight of Elijah from Jezebel, recorded in 1 Kings 19, originated about this time. The border between Israel and Jordan from 1948 to 1967 was in this area, the road was closed and Bethlehem could only be viewed from the settlement of Ramat-Rachel on the left. We now descend into the deep valley, which goes eastward to the Dead Sea. The truncated hill off to the south-east is Frank-Mountain, the ancient Herodium, where Herod the Great built himself a palace and a tomb. South of this is the site of Biblical Tekoa home of the prophet Amos.

We next reach Rachel's Tomb, a venerated shrine containing a large masonry cenotaph, which is believed to cover the place of interment of

Rachel's Tomb

the beloved wife of Jacob (Gen. 35: 16—29). Beyond Rachel's Tomb on the right is the large village of Beth-Jala identified with two other places, viz. Gallim (Isaiah 10:30, 1 Sam 25:44) and Giloh, the home of Ahitophel, (2 Sam 15:12 and Josh. 15:51).

The road now forks, that leading to the right going to Hebron. We continue into Bethlehem on the main road circling the hill and coming up to the court outside the church of The Nativity.

BETHLEHEM is one of the very early towns of Israel and in many respects is second only to Jerusalem in Biblical interest. It is the scene of many important events of Scriptural history. It was the home of Boaz and Naomi, and here was consummated the beautiful idyll of the book of Ruth. Bethlehem was the home of Jesse and David; here the latter was anointed by the Prophet Samuel; and lastly, here is the birthplace of Jesus. The Hebrew name Beth-Lehem means the "House of bread" and as its name signifies

79

Bethlehem — The Basilica of The Nativity

the district was noted in antiquity for its fruitfulness and the cultivation of its fields and terraces. In many parts of the Old Testament Bethlehem is called Ephrath, a word which means fertility; and elsewhere Bethlehem-Judah because it is situated i. the territory of the Tribe of Judah. From 1 Sam. 16 we learn that it was still the home of David's house in the early part of the 11th cent. B.C. and at this time David was called from tending his father's sheep around Bethlehem to rule over Judah and Israel.

In the early Christian period Bethlehem attracted a great number of pilgrims. The magnificent Basilica, still standing, was erected by Constantine in 330 A.D. Justinian restored its walls in the 6th century. In 600 Bethlehem was a flourishing town, holding many churches and monasteries. This prosperity ceased for a time when in 1099 the Arabs destroyed the place as the Crusading host advanced. The Franks rebuilt it but it was devastated in 1244 then rebuilt. Again it was destroyed in 1489, but during the last three centuries it was recovered from this.

The Church of the Nativity. This ancient and most interesting group of churches and monasteries, (Greek-Orthodox, Roman-Catholic and Armenian) stands over and around the rocky cave which from earliest centuries of Christendom has been held by the local inhabitants to be the Grotto connected with the inn to which Joseph and Mary went on the Eve of the first Christmas and that in which Jesus was born and where He was laid in a stone manger in which animals used to be fed. When the Emperor Constantine (first Christian emperor) decided to build a fitting place of worship in Bethlehem to commemorate the birth of Christ, his representatives naturally selected this cave as the center of the proposed Basilica.

Bethlehem — the church of The Nativity

The church is approached from the west, through the large paved courtyard. The cause for the extreme smallness of the entrance is seen above it; its proportions, which were originally adequate, have more than once been reduced, during the times of insecurity, both for safety's sake and for excluding horses and other animals, which at some times were taken inside.

The length of the interior is about 200 feet and the breadth about 50 feet. The handsome aisle columns are of reddish limestone. The roof was once beautifully gilded and painted; the north and south side walls were also covered with mosaics originally. Beautiful mosaics of Constantine's church, designed to imitate a number of carpets, are under wooden coverings at a depth of 2,5 feet below the modern floor.

The central part, with the main apse, belongs to the Greeks; the Choir is screened off by a highly ornamented wooden partition, forming an iconoclaustrum in which stands the high altar.

The Grotto, or Chapel of the Nativity, which has remained practically the same (with minor alterations) throughout its long history, underlies the central portion of the transept, from which, on either side of the raised platform, a circular staircase descends. The Grotto is 40 feet long, 12 feet wide, and 10 feet high. It is lighted by 32 lamps. The walls are lined with marble and the floor paved with the same material. In the floor under the altar in the small east apse is the Silver Star, which is said to mark the spot of the divine birth.

Opposite, three steps lead down to the Chapel of The Manger, where was the manger in which the Virgin Mother laid her child.

The northeast part of the transept of the church belongs to the Armenians. In the north apse is the entrance to the Church of St. Catherine of the Latins; a flight of steps in the south-west corner here leads down to the Chapel of The Innocents, which is a continuation of the Grotto of the Nativity

The Silver Star at the Grotto of The Nativity bearing the Latin inscription, "HIC DE VIRGINE MARIA JESUS CHRISTUS NATUS EST"

To the Shepherds' Fields, the road descends eastward through the Christian village of Beit-Sahur and nearby cultivated plain known as the FIELD OF BOAZ in which Ruth met her future husband. Soon we reach the Shepherds' Fields surrounded by a wall and containing olive trees. In the center is the Grotto of the Shep-herds, a cave, which may have been originally a cistern, but was converted into a chapel. The tradition which regards this field as that in which the "Shepherds" were "keeping watch over their flocks by night" at the time of the birth of Christ in the Inn of Bethlehem is of very ancient origin (Luke 2: 8—16).

Grotto of the Nativity

Bethlehem — General view

The Field of Boaz and the Shepherds' Fields

East of Bethlehem (seen in the background) is the field in which Ruth, as a gleaner, met her future husband. A short distance from here are the Shepherds' Fields

HEBRON

From Rachel's Tomb near Bethlehem the road continues south through the hills and District of Judea (held by Jordan 1948 to 1967 now administrated by Israel). At mile 8 we arrive at the Pools of Solomon — three enormous, well-built reservoirs in the valley, one below the other. The name "Solomon's Pools" is due to a passage of Solomon's in Ecclesiastes (2:6) "I made me pools of water, to water therewith the wood that bringeth forth trees". They may have been originally constructed during the early Jewish Monarchy. Pontius Pilate installed a water supply for Jerusalem and it is thought that he repaired these pools then.

Nearby is a large medieval castle and a caravanserai which was built in the 17th century. The main Hebron road continues south past the now rebuilt K'far-

Etzion "Block" (of Jewish settlements — Hebrew "Gush") which was destroyed in 1948. A new road leads from here to the valley of Elah. At mile 20 a roadway leads off to the left to the remarkable ruins which seem, without doubt, to mark the site of the dwelling of the Patriarch Abraham, when his abode was under the Oak of Mamre. The ruins are remains of buildings of Herod, Hadrian, Constantine, and other builders, including Arabic remains. This is probably the place where Abraham received the three angelic messengers (Gen. 18: 1-15) announcing to him that he would have a son.

Shortly before entering Hebron, on the right, was the "Well of Sirah" (2 Sam.3:26) from which Joab brought Abner back to the gate of Hebron and slew him in revenge for the death of his brother Asahel.

Hebron is a very old city. In Gen. 23:2 it is called Kiryat-Arba. Sarah, Abraham's wife died here and the Patriarch bought the field of Ephron the Hittite, with its Cave of Machpelah, for a family burying place, and in it he buried her (Gen. 23) and here Abraham himself was buried, as were also Isaac and Rebecca, Jacob and his wife Leah.

The city was destroyed by Joshua (Josh. 10 : 36—37), it was in the inheritance of the Tribe of Judah and rose to importance in the Israelite period, being one of the cities of refuge, and for seven years was David's capital. Here David's son, Absalom, was born and here he later raised the standard of rebellion against his father (2 Sam. 15 : 10) Under the Arabs in the 7th century it revived being considered as it still is, one of the sacred cities of Islam. The Mosque of Abraham, the chief interest of Hebron, is situated in the south-east part of the town. It encloses and is built over the Cave of Machpelah.

Hebron—Beer-Sheva. The road from Hebron to Beer-Sheva, widened and repaired since the Six Day War in 1967 leads south through the hills of Judea, and descends to the plains of the northern Negev, across the former border between Jordan and Israel and continues to Beer-Sheva, capital of the Negev.

Hebron — the Mosque of Abraham

The present sanctuary was built over the Cave of Macpelah containing the cenotaphs of the Patriarchs

BETHANY (Aramaic "house of poverty") is a little suburb-village situated about 1½ miles ("fifteen furlongs" — John 11:18) east of Jerusalem, on the main road leading past Gethsemane and Olivet to JERICHO and the DEAD SEA. In Jesus' time the route from Bethany to Jerusalem was a footpath over the Mount of Olives, on which the Palm Sunday procession began.

Bethany was a place to which Christ often resorted. It was the home of His friends Lazarus, Martha and Mary, and here He restored Lazarus to life (John 11:1—44). In the house of Simon the Leper, the woman anointed His feet with costly spikenard (Mark 14:3, John 12:3). The principal site is the Tomb of Lazarus, which is near the mosque, with a descent of 22 steps into the cavern leading into the tomb.

Bethany — Lazarus Tomb

Hebron — Mosque of Abraham (interior) — Cave of Machpelah

The Jericho road itself is a very historical one. It follows the course of the ancient route from the Jordan Valley, which was the boundary between the Tribes of Judah and Benjamin, and which the Jews from the northern and eastern Tribes followed when they came up to Jerusalem to attend the festivals.

At mile 12, at the height of land between Jerusalem and Jericho, we pass the Good Samaritan's Inn. Tradition has, very aptly, identified this inn with the scene of Christ's parable of "the man who fell among thieves"

The Inn of the Good Samaritan

(Luke 10: 30—37). The very steep part of the road ends at the plain of the Jordan valley. The view from here is magnificent — the Dead Sea on the right and the green belt along the Jordan, with the beautiful background of the mountains of Moab. Jericho lies in the midst of the flat plain, a real oasis. The road goes through the plain, crosses a large bridge over a brook and enters the Arab town, situated 825 feet below sea level, south-east of Elisha's Fountain and Old Testament Jericho, about 5 miles west of the Jordan

River and about 9 miles north-west of the Dead Sea.

JERICHO (meaning possibly "place of fragrance" or "moon city" — see "city of palm trees" Deut. 34:3, Judg. 1:16, 3:13) is one of the oldest occupied towns in the country and of the Middle East and has a series of sites, for it changed location after sieges, earthquakes and other catastrophes of this region.

Jericho of Old Testament times — the hillock at the base of the Mount of Temptation (Mt. Quruntul), near Elisha's Fountain whose brackish waters the prophet once healed (2 kings 2:19-22), was a Canaanite town of some importance as early as 3000 B.C. It was utterly destroyed by the Israelites in the middle of the 13th century B.C. (Josh. 6) (W.F. Albright-c. 1350, J. Garstang -1400 B.C.).

Joshua laid a curse upon the man who should rebuild the city, saying; "Cursed be the man before the Lord, that riseth up and buildeth this city Jericho, he shall lay the foundation thereof in his firstborn, and in his youngest son shall he set up the gates of it".

This site was entirely covered until 1907. In that and following years extensive excavations were conducted here, which proved to be of great interest. The whole course of the city wall has been uncovered. Its foundations were composed of un-hewn stones and upon these stood a wall of sun-dried bricks. Remains of the Canaanite walls which fell at the time of the Hebrew conquest were found.

New Testament Jericho, through which Jesus often passed en route to Jerusalem, is situated about 2 miles south of the O.T. Jericho. It was built about the time of the birth of Jesus and continued to flourish until the end of the 3rd. century, then it gradually disappeared until Arabs in the 8th century converted it into a military outpost.

Jericho's climate and vegetation are sub-tropical. It is well-watered by

Old Jericho — excavated mound

Hisham palace — mosaic floor

Jericho — General view

Elisha's Fountain and is known for its good soil and early ripening fruits- dates, oranges and bananas. In past years some modern houses were built here by Jerusalem residents for use during the winter months.

Hisham's Palace. Ruins of an 8th century palace of Arab origin, found about a mile north of old Jericho, proved to be the remains of a winter palace of the Caliph of that name.

The "Bik'ah" (valley) road through the Jordan Valley leads north, along the western bank of the Jordan River (the river is the border). It passes by newly established farming settlements, and, via the old city of Beth-She'an comes to Tiberias and the Sea of Galilee.

The Dead Sea, is about 9 miles from Jericho. It is 48 miles long — north to south and 10 miles wide at its widest point. Its area is about 360 sq. miles; max. depth 1310 feet. Its shores are the lowest parts of the earth's surface — 1292 feet below sea level and 3786 feet lower than Jerusalem.

The salinity of the Dead Sea water is four to five times that of ocean water, that is, 23 to 25 per cent of salts against 4 to 6 per cent in ocean water. Analysis discloses the following mineral contents : Chlorine — 67% Bromine — 1.98%, Sulphate — 0.22%, Sodium — 10.20%, Potassium — 1.60% Calcium — 1.51%, Magnesium — 16.80%.

The Dead Sea

Qumran caves

Qumran ruins

QUMRAN. The ruins of the settlement of Qumran, where the famous **Dead Sea Scrolls** were found by Bedouin shepherds in 1947, are on a hill overlooking the north-west shore of the Dead Sea. Near the cliffs on an alluvial plateau is the site of an ancient building complex comprising a main building, about 111 feet long by about 90 feet wide, constructed of large stone squares coated with plaster. There has evidently been a dining room, kitchens, cisterns, a dormitory, workshops, swimming pools and, most interesting of all, a scriptorium — the writing table which was of masonry, which had apparently fallen through a collapsed floor from an upper room. The site was thoroughly excavated over several seasons, and has yielded important data about the nature, size, and date of the Qumran community: — within the limits of 140 B.C. and 67 A.D. The number of living there at any one time was in the neighborhood of two to four hundred. The fresh water springs at **Ein-Feshkha**, about 2 miles south, were probably used for the growing of crops and other needs of the community.

Identified with the Essenes, a sect of Judaism described by Josephus and Philo, it is known from their literature that the people of Qumran were Jews who split off from Jerusalem or main stream of Judaism. The life of the community was largely asceptic, and their practices included ritual bathing, sometimes referred to as baptism.

One of the scholars who recognized the antiquity of the **Dead Sea Scrolls** was the late Prof. Eleazar L. Sukenik of the Hebrew University of Jerusalem, who was subsequently successful in purchasing some of them. The Scrolls and other findings from the caves of Qumran and the area are at the Israel Museum's Shrine of the Book and at the Rockefeller Museum in Jerusalem.

EIN-GEDI

A newly constructed road along the western shore of the Dead Sea leads

Ein Gedi Oasis

south and arrives at the Oasis (and farming settlement) of Ein-Gedi (Heb. "Kid's Fountain") whither David withdrew in his flight from Saul (1 Samuel 24:1-2). Ein Gedi was one of the ancient cities of Judea and finds frequent mention in the Bible. In the days of Solomon it was famed for its fragrant camphire. The Song of Songs (of Solomon) 1:4 says : my beloved is unto me as a cluster of camphire in the vineyards of Ein-Gedi".

Ein Gedi's Inn, with its nicely run self-service restaurant is operated by the members of Kibbutz Ein-Gedi near the well kept Dead Sea bathing beach. The road continues south and arrives at the foot of the fortress-hill of **Masada**, from where cable-cars are operated over the "Snake-path" to the top of the hill.

Ein Gedi's inn

MASADA (Hebrew: fortress) was built, according to Josephus Flavius the historian, by Herod the Great in about 36 B.C. who *"built a wall of white stone around the whole top of the hill, seven ris (stadia) long, twelve cubits high and eight cubits wide; and on the wall all around he built thirty-seven towers...the lesser buildings were built on the inside..."* This immense rock (area of the upper plateau — about 20 acres), was scene of one of the most remarkable and tragic last stands for independence made by the Jews against the Romans. Its fall, in 73 A.D. marked the end of that independence until 1948.

Jonathan Maccabeus was the first to build a fortress on this rock. Herod fled to it in 42 B.C. when the Parthians took Jerusalem. A few years later he enclosed the plateau by a wall, built defence towers and constructed an elaborate palace on the northeastern corner: It is said that Herod prepared this fortress as a refuge in time of need against two dangers which he always envisaged: the one, that the Jewish people might depose him and put a king from the royal house which had reigned before him on the throne; and the second, even worse than the first, the fear of Cleopatra, Queen of Egypt...*"Herod hewed large caverns in the side of the rock for reservoirs and linked them by an aqueduct to a nearby gorge which channeled the water during the rainy season...and in that manner he was able to provide water for those living there as though there were springs at their disposal..."*

After Herod's death, Masada was held for his son Archelaus, and had a Roman Garrison. From 6 to 66 A.D. it was a Roman post. A band of Zealots took Masada by surprise in the very first days of the Great Revolt. There they found the arms that made their leader Menachem a "veritable king" in the party strife for Jerusalem. When Menachem was killed, his nephew Ele'azar managed to withdraw to Masada.

After the conquest and destruction of Jerusalem by the Romans in 70 A.D., a band of Jewish patriots led by Ele'azar Ben-Yair determined to continue the struggle for freedom and withdrew to Masada for another and even more hopeless stand. They were followed by Roman Legionairs under the command of Falvius Silva, a lieutenant of Titus, who opened large scale siege operations. For many months the Romans tried to storm the fortress but were beaten back. Under cover of weapons which outranged the bows and spears of the defenders they constructed a ramp of beaten earth and stones on the western side of Masada. Their battering ram and siege engines were brought almost to the edge of the plateau and breached Herod's wall. The defenders countered by building an inner wall, consisting of earth encased in wood. Flavius Silva then ordered it set on fire. This was the beginning of the end. Josephus Flavius describes the heroic end of Masada in his "Wars of the Jews": *"When the inner wall burnt, Ele'azar gathered his men and urged them, rather than fall into the hands of their enemy, to die by their own hands...they then chose ten men by lot out of them to slay all the rest, every one of whom lay himself down by his wife and children on the ground, and threw his arms about them, and they offered their necks to the stroke of those who by lot executed that melacholy office, and when these ten had, without fear, slain them all, they made the same rule of casting lots for themselves, that he whose lot it was should kill the other nine, and after all should kill himself..."*

Flavius Josephus adds and concludes that the Romans could only *"wonder at the courage of their resolution and the immovable concept of death, which so great a number of them had shown, when they went through with such an action as that was..."*

The fortress hill of Masada

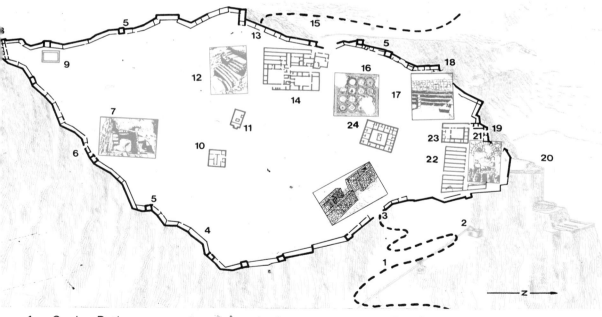

1. Snake Path
2. Cable-car
3. Snake Path gate
4. Eastern wall
5. Tower
6. Southern gate
7. Ritual bath
8. Southern citadel

9. Great pool
10. Building No. XII
11. Building No. XI
12. Swimming pool
13. Head of western stairs
14. Western palace
15. Western path
16. Byzantine church

17. Synagogue
18. Scrolls' casemate
19. Water Gate
20. Northern palace
21. Bathhouse
22. Store rooms
23. Building No. VII
24. Officers quarters

Masada — water cisterns

Masada — the synagogue

ELE'AZAR'S ORATION

"My loyal followers, long ago we resolved to serve neither the Romans nor anyone else but only God, who alone is the true and righteous Lord of men : now the time has come that bids us prove our determination by our deeds. At such a time we must not disgrace ourselves : hitherto we have never submitted to slavery even when it brought no danger with it : we must not choose slavery now, and with it penalties that will mean the end of everything if we fall alive into the hands of the Romans. For we were the first of all to revolt, and shall be the last to break off the struggle. And I think it is God who has given us this privilege, that we can die nobly and as free men, unlike others who were unexpectedly defeated. In our case it is evident that day-break will end our resistance, but we are free to choose an honourable death with our loved ones. This our enemies cannot prevent, however earnestly they may pray to take us alive; nor can we defeat them in battle."

"Let our wives die unabused, our children without knowledge of slavery : after that, let us do each other an ungrudging kindness, preserving our freedom as a glorious winding-sheet. But first let our

possessions and the whole fortress go up in flames : it will be a bitter blow to the Romans, that I know, to find our persons beyond their reach and nothing left for them to loot. One thing only let us spare — our store of food : it will bear witness when we are dead to the fact that we perished, not through want but because, as we resolved at the beginning, we chose death rather than slavery."

The road from Masada continues south along the shore of the Dead Sea, passes by Ein-Bokek with its nice hotels and well kept bathing beach, and past "Hamei-Zohar" (hotel, sulphur springs, spa, bathing beach) it comes to "Shefech-Zohar" near Mt. Sodom (for new Arabah road, via Sodom to Eilat — see page 96).

S'DOM (Sodom) is at the southern end of the Dead Sea. In no region on earth, it has been said, have nature and history, in climatic meeting, set so awesome a stage for so tragic a drama as at Sodom. Here, at 1290 feet below sea level and lowest point on earth, was enacted before man the classic and terrible judgement on human sin: *"The Lord rained upon Sodom and upon Gomorrah brimstone and fire... and He overthrew those cities, and all the plain, and all the inhabitants of the cities and that which grew upon the ground..."* (Gen. 19:24-25).

No more majestic theatre could be conceived for so spectacular an event. At the center of this gigantic natural rift between two mountain ranges lies the stretch of water of the Dead Sea. Its surface a fullbodied blue, glistening

Masada — Watergate...

in the rays of the hot sun, smooth, still and serene for most of the year. Sodom in its earlier existence symbolized vice. In its fiery destruction it became the symbol of the standard judgment of sin, much quoted by the prophets of old in thunderous warning to the people to mend their ways.

Ascending the hills near "Shefech-Zohar", the road leads to the newly built town of Arad. The scene from the top is one of stately grandeur, height set against depth, the blue of the water against tawny crag and rock and in the eastern distance, the upward sweep of the mountains of Moab.

The road ascends the barren hills and comes to the new town of **Arad** which was established in 1961 on the heights, over 2000 feet above sea level, 18 miles from the Dead Sea. Well-planned, fast growing modern Arad, known for its dry, cool air, has nice hotels and a large shopping center.

The main road continues through the vast plain of the northern Negev, past many Bedouin camps and settlements. A large whitish mound seen from the road, on the right, marks the site of **Biblical Arad** (Num. 21:1-2; Josh. 12, 14; Judg. 1,16) which was excavated by archaeologists.

TO JERUSALEM VIA HEBRON, a road, reopened and repaired after the

Masada — Herod's northern palace
(lower terrace)

Six Day War in 1967, leads across the former border with Jordan, through the Judean mountains, via Hebron and Bethlehem to Jerusalem.

BEER-SHEVA ("Well of oath") was in Biblical days a favourite dwelling place of the Hebrew Patriarchs (Gen. 21:31). Paths from all directions and people of most diverse backgrounds and cultures have met in Beer-Sheva from the start of the story of civilization. "From Dan even to Beer-Sheva" (Judg. 20:1) has become a classic phrase for the North-South limits of Israel. Beer-Sheva today is a modern city and Capital of the Negev with a population of about 130,000.

Negev landscape

Bedouin girls

THE NEGEV ("the dry") is the southern part of Israel. Because of its geographical position in relation to Judea, this area became known as "the south." Throughout Bible times grazing was the main occupation in the Negev, trees were highly prized. It is a land of sharp contrasts, of surprising fertility extreme barrenness, of rain in scarcity and cisterns without number, of extreme dryness and heavy dew, of cultivable plains and innumerable dry stream beds that on rare occasions are hosts to short-lived torrents, where sturdy pioneers seek once again to strike root.

Between the 4th and 7th centuries A.D. successful efforts were made to occupy and cultivate the Negev. Extensive ruins of water systems, reservoirs, cisterns, and ruins of many formerly inhabited places testify to the extensive civilization current here in this period.

Bedouin tent

Waiting for a lift...

Transport is coming...

TO EILAT
AND THE
RED SEA

* **From Sodom and Dead Sea via New Arabah Road**

* **From Beer-Sheva via old road and Mitzpeh-Ramon**

* **From Eilat to Sharm E-Sheikh**

* **Sinai, St. Catherine Monastery, Shivta — Subeita**

"Lot's Wife" — Sodom

The Dead Sea

TO EILAT AND THE RED SEA

1. The Arabah (Aravah) road;

From "Shefekh Zohar" near the southern shore of the Dead Sea the road continues south and follows the base of "Mt. Sodom" — a mountain of solid salt rock. A pillar on Mt. Sodom with a vague outline of a human figure is called **"Lot's Wife"**. Proceeding, the road passes by the large plants of the **Israel Potash Works**, where potash and other minerals are extracted from the Dead Sea's water. The road continues through the plain, ascends the hills and soon arrives at a junction from where the new Arabah road, leading via Hatzevah to Eilat begins. Ascending the steep hills from the junction, the road leads via Dimona to Beer-Sheva.

2. The "old road" via Mitzpeh-Ramon;

The "old road" to Eilat leads south from Beer-Sheva along the pre-1948 highway from Palestine to Egypt through Sinai. It passes by the settlement of Mash'abei-Sadeh, close to Kibbutz Revivim, and continues past Shivta to the pre-1967 border post of Nitzana (Auja el-Hafir). A route from Nitzana leads south, past Bir-Birein (Beerotayim) to Quseima and Ein-Qudeirat; about 10 miles further south it comes to Ein-Kadeis or Qadesh, identified with **Biblical Kadesh-Barnea**, the central camp site of Israel during their Wilderness wanderings. Situated at the north eastern part of Sinai, between the Wilderness of Paran and the Wilderness of Zin, some 70 miles south of Hebron, Kadesh-Barnea was the camp from where observers were sent by Moses to spy out the land (Num. 13:21-26 — see page 3).

Turning left, off the Nitzana highway, the road leads through the barren hills of the Negev and comes to Kibbutz S'de-Boker which gained fame as "Ben-Gurion's settlement" in the desert — now green and blooming. Ben-Gurion's hut, the former home of Israel's great leader at S'de-Boker is now open for visits by the public.

David and Paula Ben-Gurion are buried at the nearby agricultural highschool south of Kibbutz S'de Boker.

The main road continues south through the undulating emptiness of the Negev. A rough track branches off to the left and goes to the edge of Nahal Zin, one of the Negev's most striking canyons. In olden days the great "Sultan's Route" followed it down to the Arabah wilderness. A steep path down comes to Ein Zin (Ein Avdat, or Ein Murrah in Arabic), a hidden spring with crystal-clear rock pool.

S'de-Boker — Tombs of David and Paula Ben-Gurion (left)
The tombs are at the Agricultural College, about two miles south of Kibbutz S'de Boker — overlooking the grandiose canyon of "Nahal Zin", the eastern part of the Biblical Wilderness of Zin (Josh. 15:1; Num. 34:3)

Avdat — ruins

Kibbutz S'de-Boker — Ben- Gurion's Home

AVDAT of the Nabateans and Byzantines, once the distant goal of full-fledged desert expeditions is soon seen on the left. It was an important post station on the road to Eilat. The Nabateans were the relatives of the Idumeans and their successors in the possession of the Negev. They were a nation of Caravan traders, whose kingdom straddled the southern highway from Arabia to the Mediterranean. From Ceylon and India, from Southern Arabia, the cargoes of spices and silk, of emeralds and incense, were carried overland by the Nabateans to the Mediterranean coast. The caravan traffic was by no means, one way.

Their occupation of the Araba wilderness up to the Dead Sea made them the most important salt-purveyors of a sub-continent.

The Nabatean cities of the Negev were occupied in the 1st century A.D. by the Romans whose garrisons guarded the trade routes from Egypt to Syria and from Ashkelon to Eilat. Modern archeological surveys have discovered surprisingly high number of Nabatean sites in the Negev, of which five cities, the "Negev Pentapolis" survived until the Arab conquest. They are Khalutza, Shivta, Avdat, Nitzana and Kurnub (Mamshit-Mempsis).

Ruins of Avdat in the Negev — view from the air
The Nabatean cave-dwellings seen on the slopes were abandoned in the era of the Byzantine occupation. The partly restored remains of the Byzantine town are on the high plateau of the hill. An old Roman map (Tabula) marks Avdat as an important post station on the road to Eilat. This road followed the northern rim of the Ramon crater (further south) and from there it descended south-east into the Arabah (Aravah) and reached Ein Ghadian, now identified with Biblical Yotvata, about 25 miles north of Eilat.

Avdat — Byzantine church

With the ascent to the hill-top, the ruins of Avdat change in character. It is improbable that the Nabatean cave dwellings were abandoned in the era of Byzantine occupation. The road reaches the plateau near a small quarter of fairly large and well built houses which formed an Eastern suburb of the fortified town, consisting of a fort and monastery only. This quarter, where the officers of the garrison and the rich merchants lived, was protected by the continuous outer walls of buildings and gardens. The fortress on the upper plateau is the best preserved and most impressive feature of the ruined town, a long rectangle whose heavy ashlar walls with square corner towers and projecting bastions enclose a wide area.

Looking down from the acropolis, one sees the wide and flat bottom of the valley criss-crossed by the surviving Tamarisk hedges of the Byzantine fields. The soil has remained intact, and the dams which once stored rains in the gorge that comes in from the north, could be repaired with little effort.

The main road continues south and, gradually ascending the hills, comes to the settlement of Mitzpeh-Ramon, situated on a conical hill, crowned by enormous rock cubes (913 meters — about 2800 feet - above sea level) overlooking the gigantic area of the Ramon Crater (Hebrew: Makhtesh). The colosal arena of Ramon, about 21 by 7 miles, is surrounded by a moonscape of mountain peaks.

Descending into the crater, the road passes by the gypsum quarries and continues through the wild and barren plains and hills. It finally descends from the heights of the Negev plateau and joins with the new Sodom-Eilat highway running along the mountains of Edom, through the plain of the Araba. From here to Eilat the distance is 33 miles. The road passes near the new settlement of Ketura (right) and Grofit (left) and comes to the settlement of Yotvata, established in the wilderness in 1951.

The oasis of Yotvata (Yothbatha — "a land of rivers of water" Num.33:33-34 Deut.10:7) was one of the stations of the Israelites on their way from Egypt to Canaan. Remains of a Solomonic fortress were discovered here on the top of a hill near the spring. It guarded the access to some of the most important copper and iron mines at nearby Timna, which had been intensively exploited by King Solomon, and it commanded the main highway on the west side of the Araba rift to and from his chief seaport, Ezion-geber: Eilat, on the Red Sea.

The settlers of the blossoming settlement of Yotvata have planted groves of date palms and orchards of other fruits and their irrigated fields are yielding abundant harvests of various crops. A "Milk Bar" run by members of Yotvata is near the road. A fenced area, about a mile from here called "Hai-bar" is a game preserve.

To "King Solomon's Pillars" a road branches off the highway and leads west through a haunted valley, guarded by malachite, blood-coloured and tigerstriped hills, some of which, the winds and erosion have carved to look like towering statues and idols. The road ends at the huge red cliffs called "Solomon's Pillars".

KING SOLOMON'S MINES are at Timna, some 15 miles north of Eilat. An amazing number of large copper-mining and smelting centers have been found in the Araba by Nelson Glueck, with slag heaps, ruins of workmen's quarters and towns, flues for draughts up the deep valleys and furnaces producing metal in the 10th century B.C. helping build up the fabulous wealth of Solomon.

The king's own industrial and shipping center at Ezion-geber at the head of the Gulf of Eilat (Aqabah) was excavated by Glueck, exploring from 1932 for several seasons. The Hebrew king had at Ezion-geber (I Kings 9:26) a port for exporting metal, the proceeds from which bought luxury wares for his court and ornaments for the Temple which Hiram of Tyre and his craftsmen helped build in Jerusalem. Some of the slag heaps are spotted with green, from copper never refined out of it.

The excavations of this important industrial center of the Hebrew Monarchy yielded an elaborate complex of masonry of the 10th century B.C. port. The queen of Sheba, whether she came by ship or caravan, must have rested at Ezion-Geber-Eilat before she went up to Jerusalem.

"King Solomon Pillars"

Eilat — General view

EILAT Until the Six Day War in 1967, Eilat was the southernmost point in Israel. The modern Israeli town of Eilat, port and gateway to Africa and the Far East has no ancient history at all, it just did not exist before Israel became a state in 1948. During the British Mandate a little police station stood here at the waterless site of Um-Rash rash, between Aqabah in Jordan and the Egyptian Sinai.

EILAT (Elath, Eloth — "the great trees", palms or some other sacred trees) was a name of a place at the north-east corner of the Gulf of Aqabah, passed by the Israelites on their way from Sinai (Deut. 2:8). It was near Ezion-geber and in the two centuries between David and Uzziah it passed back and forth between Edomites and Israelites (2 Kings 14:22, 16:6). It was coveted as a strategic resting place for caravans on the great Spice Route out of Arabia and as the merchandising port for Solomon's commerce in copper mined in the Araba.

Eilat today is a thriving town and great tourist center. It is a paradise for "amphibian" people and its beautiful beaches are inviting. Many luxury hotels were built around the Gulf's shore set into the mountain frame. Aqabah in Jordan, of "Lawrence of Arabia" fame, the shores of Saudi Arabia, and Sinai are all within close, view from any point here. Population of almost 20,000, the port, fishing, shopping centers, restaurants, desert tours, sails by glass-bottomed boats, a new, unique, under-sea aquarium, excursions to Sinai and more — this is Eilat, a "must" for every Israeli as well as tourists and visitors from all corners of the world.

Eilat — View from the east

Eilat — Laromme Hotel

Eilat — hotels on the beach

Bedouins with camels for hire

Eilat — Undersea World Observatory and Aquarium

Coral Island — off shore, south of Eilat

The "Fjord", south of Eilat

Road to Sharm Esheikh

Sinai — landscape

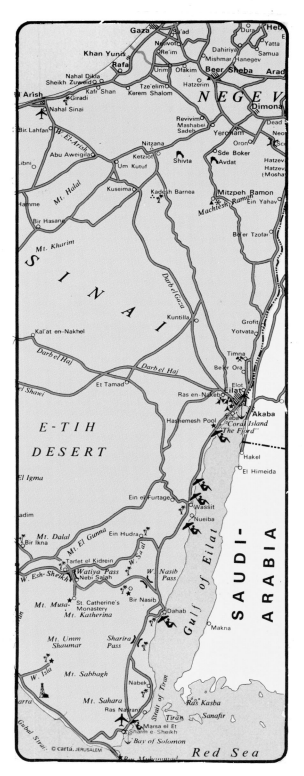

FROM EILAT TO SHARM E-
SHEIKH (distance — 145 miles), the
road continues past "Coral Island"
and the so-called "Fjord" and, following the shore of the Gulf comes to
Nuweiba, renamed (Heb.) "Nevi'ot" —
a new settlement — a lovely resort
with a beautiful sandy beach, motel,
restaurant, gas station, etc. (45 miles
from Eilat). Proceeding, the road now
ascends the hills, continues through
mountainous eastern Sinai, follows
the so-called "9th Brigade Track"
(named so after the courageous break-
through of the famous Israeli 9th
Brigade on its way to Sharm E-Sheikh
in 1956) and reaches the crossroad of
Dahab (Hebrew: "Di-Zahav") —
another new settlement — a beautiful
resort with palm trees on the Gulf's
shore, 44 miles from Nuweiba. The
road continues through the Sharrira
Pass, descends back to the coast and
arrives, past Ras-Nasrani — overlooking the island and Straits of Tiran —
at Sharm E-Sheikh — Ophira (Dahab-
Sharm Esheikh — 45 miles).

Neviot (Nueibah) — the oasis and beach

Straits of Tiran

Sharm Esheikh — Bay of Naama

Bedouin children in Sinai

"Duo Sinai" — Daily Concerts near Straits of Tiran

Dahab — Di-Zahav — the bay

"Kennedy's head" — Sharm Esheikh

SHARM E-SHEIKH (Arabic: the Sheikh's Bay; Hebrew: Ophira), at the southern tip of the Sinai Peninsula is a small new settlement which made world headlines in 1967 when the nearby Strait of Tiran was closed by Egypt to prevent Israeli shipping between the port of Eilat and the Red Sea. It has several charming little bays with beautiful beaches for swimming and vacationing.

FROM SHARM E-SHEIKH TO ST. CATHERIN'S MONASTERY

A road leads past Ras-Muhammed along the shore of the Gulf of Suez to the old fishing port-town of At-Tour—a former Egyptian quarantine station for pilgrims going to Mecca in Arabia. From here a route goes via Firan to St. Catherine's Monastery at the foot of Mt. Moses (Mt. Sinai — Mt. Horeb, Arabic: Jebal Mussa) (see page 69 — Sinai).

THE RED SEA

The Red Sea separates the continents of Asia and Africa. It is about 1200 miles long, from Bab-el-Mandeb where it joins with the Indian Ocean, to Sharm-E-Sheikh where its two "arms", the gulfs of Suez and Eilat (Aqabah), begin. On its Asian shore are Saudi-Arabia, Yemen, Israel and Jordan, and on its opposite, African shore, are Egypt, Sudan, Ethiopia and Somaliland.

THE GULF OF SUEZ, the Red Sea's north-west arm, separates Egypt from the Sinai Peninsula. It is about 190 miles long, about 30 miles wide and about 280 feet deep. Its northern "extension" forms the Suez Canal, which connects the Red Sea with the Mediterranean.

THE GULF OF EILAT (Aqabah) is another arm of the Red Sea and is narrow and very deep. Its length, between the island of Tiran and Eilat, is 112 miles and its widest part does not exceed 15 miles. Its great depth begins close to its shore, reaching a depth of about 6000 feet at its center.

THE EILAT — S'DOM NEW ARABA HIGHWAY leads north through the wild plain of the Araba (Arava), between the mountains of Edom (in Jordan, on the right) and the mountains of the Negev (on the left). It passes by the pioneering border settlements of Paran, Nahal Zofar, Ein-Yahav and Hatzeva and ends near the Dead Sea, where it joins with the road coming from S'dom (Sodom) and leading via Dimona and Nevatim to Beer Sheva: from the Gulf of Eilat (Red Sea) to S'dom (Dead Sea) the distance is 131 miles).

Bedouin children in Sinai

Hatzevah Road Inn

107

MAP OF THE SINAI PENINSULA — "INTERIM AGREEMENT" LINES

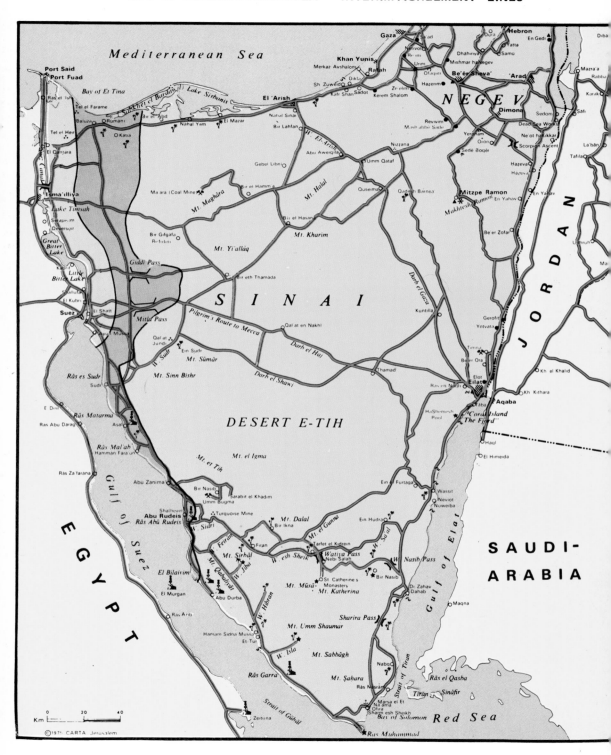

SINAI

The Sinai Peninsula is a 260 mile-long triangle at whose southern apex the Gulf of Eilat (Aqabah) joins the Gulf of Suez at the head of the Red Sea. Its inverted base extends 150 miles along the Mediterranean. Before the Six Day War in 1967, Sinai formed the border between Egypt and Israel, with the actual border line being near the so-called Gaza Strip, close to Ashkelon in southern Israel. From 1967 until the "Yom Kippur" War on October 6th 1973, the Suez Canal and Gulf became and were the cease-fire line and border between the two countries. Following the "Yom Kippur War" and the "Disengagement of troops" agreement signed by Egypt and Israel, and following heavy fighting and long negotiations, new cease-fire lines, a few miles east of the Suez Canal were established. On June 5th 1975 the Suez Canal was reopened by Egypt and on September 1st, an additional "Interim Agreement" was signed, following which the Abu-Rudeis oil fields were handed back to Egypt by Israel and the Israeli Army withdrew to the east side of the Mitla and Giddi Passes (see map on opposite page —108).

The Sinai Peninsula is characterized by extraordinary beauty of line and colour, with granite peaks rising 8000 feet above sea level. Sinai has three types of terrain; a) a 15-mile wide band of sandy dunes reaching south from the Mediterranean; b) a high plateau of limestone and gravel intersected by dry streambeds and running 150 miles south of the sand belt; c) a granite mountainous mass reaching 8000 feet above sea level at the apex of the triangle peninsula.

GEOLOGY. Sinai is surrounded in the west by the Gulf of Suez and in the east by the very deep depression of the Gulf of Eilat, which is part and an extension of the "Great Rift". In respect of both — geology and geomorphology — the peninsula is divided into two main areas: the northern part covers about three quarters of its entire area, consisting mostly of sedimentary rocks, mainly cretaceous and hanterivian of the cenomanian period until the Eocene. In general, the strata shows a slight inclination towards the north. The landscape is one of great plains, cut by wide and not very deep river-beds, with dominant colours ranging from yellow to brown. The southern part consists of crystalline magamatic (metamorphic) rock. The oldest rock formations found in Sinai are metamorphic, outstanding in their dark colours.

Towards the end of the metamorphosic folding, the area underwent a general uplift followed by an alluvial period. Thereafter came a new period of extremely intense volcanic activity. The formation of volcanic strata extended over a depth of more than 1000 meters (3,300 feet). The top of "Mt. Moses" (Jebal Moussa) is itself a volcanic col; the filled crater of a volcano from which erupted at least part of the lava that now forms "Mt. Catherine". More than two thirds of the area of the precamberian mountain-mass consists of granitic rock, formed over a period of more than 100 million years. The south part of the Sinai peninsula is rich with many diversified "Dayeks". The "Dayek", dark-green in colour, is an elongated rock which originally penetrated in a liquid form into a rock fissure and then widened the cleft when solidifying.

SAINT CATHERINE MONASTERY was founded in the third century and by the 4th century it housed a great number of monks. Tradition has it that the monastery was built exactly at the spot where the Lord ordered Moses to take his people out of Egypt (Exodus 3:1—12) During the first centuries of the Christian era, there were about 6000—7000 monks in Sinai. Their number decreased to about 300—400 during the Middle Ages. Part of them lived as hermits outside the monastery. Subsequently the number of monks fell rapidly, and today there are only 12 monks at the monastery, living and working independently, each to his own. Bedouins who live with their families in huts and caverns in the vicinity are engaged in cultivation and the keeping of the monastery's soil and gardens.

The church of the Aureola stands in the center of the monastery. It has wooden, bas-relief doors and a very valuable mosaic apsis, depicting the Aureole of Jesus. The plan of the church dates back to Emperor Justinian's times (7th century) and, like the church of the Nativity in Bethlehem, has served as a place of worship since it was built. One aisle of the church stands presumably on the exact spot of the Burning Bush. The crypt of St. Catherine is located near the central altar of the church. The tradition of Saint Catherine, patron-saint of the monastery, goes back to the 4th century, when during the reign of Maxentius Caesar (307—313), the saint, originally from Alexandria, went into a rocky valley in Sinai to devote her life to God and to escape persecution by Caesar. After pursuit, sufferings and torture Catherine was beheaded.

In 1844 Count Tischendorf found the famous Codex Sinaiticus at the monastery's library. Scientific research of that Codex proved that the Bible has been handed down, throughout the ages, very faithfully.

THE BEDOUIN tribes in Sinai are divided into two main groups: the southern and northern groups. The southern tribes are called "A-Tuara", which means "the mountaineers", "tur" being the Arabic word for a mountain. The northern tribes are called "A-Tiaha", or "the roving"; these tribes live on the plateau and in the plains. In the south, Bedouins have lived since the 13th century, coming originally from the Hedjaz in Arabia. They consist of six tribes: 1. E-Sawalha, 2. El-Uleikat, 3. El-Emzeina, 4. El-Kararsha, 5. E-Jabaliya and 6. Awlad Sa'id. The El-Emzeina tribe lives on

St. Catherine's Monastery in Sinai

the shore of the Gulf of Eilat, at the southern part of the peninsula. Its center is at Nuweiba, stretching out as far as Sharm E-Sheikh. They own the palm groves at Dahab and their main occupation is fishing.

The E-Jabaliya tribe descends from a group of about 200 Christian slaves, sent to Sinai by the Emperor Justinian who built the St. Catherine's monastery. They came originally from Volchiya in Roumania and from Alexandria, and during the Arab conquest were converted to Islam. They continue to serve the monastery and cultivate its soil and gardens, in addition to their leading of pilgrims and visitors to Mt. Moses' top.

* * * *

President Jimmy Carter of the U.S.A., **President Anwar el-Sadat** of Egypt and **Prime Minister Menachem Begin** of Israel were the signatories of the Peace Treaty between Egypt and Israel, signed in Washington on March 26, 1979.

As of 5:27 p.m., on Wednesday, April 25, Israel and Egypt are formally at peace after the exchange of the formal instruments of ratification — which are the final (or almost final) documents necessary for the peace treaty signed between the two countries to become effective. The ceremony of the exchange was held at the U.S. early-warning station at Umm-Khashiba in Sinai.

In nine months, the IDA (Israel Defence Army) has to complete its withdrawal to the El-Arish—Ras-Muhammad line in Sinai. Israel's complete withdrawal from Sinai, taken during the Six Day War of June 1967, will be completed by April 25, 1982 (see stages of withdrawal in map on Page 7). The Date of May 27, 1979 has been fixed, at the time of printing of this book, for the handing over of the town of El-Arish by Israel to Egypt. A road to northern Sinai leads south from Ashkelon, via, or past the Gaza Strip, through the western Negev and past the settlement of Kerem Shalom ("Vinyard of peace"). It continues via the former, pre-1967 border, past the new settlements of Sadot, Dikla and Yammit, which are to be evacuated by Israel in accordance with the peace treaty. The road continues through the former battlefields of the war and arrives at the town of El-Arish, capital of Sinai on the shore of the Mediterranean, near the biblical "Valley" or "River of Egypt".

Many inhabitants of El-Arish cultivate large date-palm groves on one of the world's oldest highways — the Way of the "Land of the Philistines", used by Pharaoh and modern conquerors. El-Arish was the Roman Rhinocorura and an early Roman See.

THE TEN COMMANDMENTS

I AM THE LORD
thy God, thou shalt have no other gods before me

THOU SHALT NOT
make unto thee any graven image

THOU SHALT NOT
take the name of the Lord thy God in vain

REMEMBER THE SABBATH
to keep it holy

HONOUR THY FATHER
and thy mother

THOU SHALT NOT KILL

THOU SHALT NOT
commit adultery

THOU SHALT NOT STEAL

THOU SHALT NOT
bear false witness

THOU SHALT NOT COVET
. . . anything which is thy neighbour's

SHIVTA — SUBEITA is the best preserved and most striking looking of all the Nabatean-Byzantine cities in the Negev. It owes its comparatively good preservation to the fact that it is somewhat off the major tracks and is not close enough to Gaza and Beer-Sheva to have served building contractors as an easy source of ready-shaped, stones, as her dead sister cities did many years ago.

Shivta lies off the main road leading from Beer-Sheva (35 miles) to Nitzana and Sinai. Coming upon it suddenly, it seems too dramatic to be real, too massive and majestic in appearance to have had any solid connection with the empty desert background of its setting — a true Byzantine Pompei.

There is no Nabatean stratum at Shivta. It is assumed that that earlier settlement was probably about 2 miles east of the Byzantine town. The latter was small, 1500 feet by 1200 feet and of irregular shape, with no proper circumvallation, but the walls of private houses and gardens along its outskirts are continuous and form a

Shivta (Subeita) — Byzantine church

complete girdle. This form of fortification is often found in the older Jewish villages of the country, which for serious defence relied on their main buildings, as Shivta did on its three large, well-built monasteries.

The Nabatean cities of the Negev were re-occupied by Roman garrisons in the 1st. century A.D. The last tombstones at Shivta date from about 20 years after the Arab conquest in the first half of the 7th century.

FROM JERUSALEM TO GALILEE

* Through the "West Bank" and Samaria to Galilee and the north
* The Jezreel-Esdraelon Valley, Mt. Tabor, Cana of Galilee
* Tiberias, the Sea of Galilee, the Jordan River
* The Mount of Beatitudes, Tabgha, Capernaum
* Kinneret, the Jordan Valley, Beth-She'an, Beth-Alfa, Belvoir
* Ginossar, Upper Galilee, Huleh Valley and Golan Heights

The Valley of Jezreel-Esdraelon — view from Mt. Tabor

1. THROUGH THE "WEST-BANK" & SAMARIA TO GALILEE

Taking the Nablus (Shechem) road which goes north from old Jerusalem we cross the height of land at Mt. Scopus. Stop for a minute to look back at an exceptional view of the city and surroundings and for some time to follow the watershed, through what was the Tribe of Benjamin. About 2 miles further we pass the village of Sha'fat identified with **NOB,** the home of the Priests (1 Sam. 21 : 1). The Tabernacle was stationed here in the time of Saul.

The hill on the right called Tel El Full is the old fortress of Gibeah and the chief city of Benjamin (Judg. 19 : 12) also birthplace and residence of Saul — the first king of Israel. The American School for Oriental Research has excavated four different fortresses on the summit, each built over the ruins of the preceding : the first dates from the time of the Judges, the second from the reign of Saul, the third was a boundary fort of the Ten Tribes and the latest from the time of the Maccabees. The town lay on the north slopes of the hill. To the east of this hill can be seen the village of Anathoth — home of Jeremiah.

To the west (left) on the horizon is seen Nebi-Samwil with its minaret which until recent years has been accepted as the ancient Mizpah where the prophet Samuel judged Israel for 20 years. Many learned authorities today, however, place ancient Mizpah at Tel En Nasbeh on the Nablus road south of Ramalla. Mizpah was a place of great importance in early O.T. history and when Jerusalem was destroyed by Nebuchadnezzar this became the residence of the governor of Judea, Gedaliah, appointed by the conqueror. At mile 4 on the left can be seen the traces of the old Roman road leading westwards to Antipatris — the route doubtless followed by St. Paul. The same road also goes to

Emmaus — remains of Roman road

EMMAUS which was the **"Sabbath's Day Journey"** from Jerusalem, sixty furlongs (Luke 24:13).

At mile 6 is the village of Er-Ram on a hill to the right, which undoubtedly is ancient RAMAH of Benjamin, the birthplace and home of Samuel (1 Sam. 1 : 19, Judg. 4 : 5, 1 Kings 15 : 17). It was later a frontier town between the kingdoms of Judah and Israel.

The road ahead passes near the Jerusalem airport and the village of Kalandia. Further at mile 9 on the left is a prominent long hill called Tel-En Nasbeh believed to be Mizpah of Benjamin.

The fine out-spread town before us is Ramalla which is mostly Christian On the right we enter the large Arab village of Bireh, which tradition reputes to be the "day's journey" from Jerusalem, at which Joseph and Mary missed their 12 year old son, Jesus, on their return to Nazareth (Luke 2 : 43—52). Bireh is identified with ancient Beeroth (Josh. 9:17 2 Sam. 4 : 2, 3).

About a mile further beyond Bireh a road on the right leads to ancient **BETHEL** near today's Arab village of Beitin. It was at Bethel that Jacob had his nightly vision of the ladder ascending to heaven (Gen. 28: 10-20). when Abraham first entered Canaan he pitched his tent here between Bethel and Ai (Gen. 12 : 8). South-east of Bethel is the great mound of ruins called Et-Tell — ancient Ai which was ambushed and destroyed by Joshua (Josh. 8 : 28). The prominent mountain in the distance to the north-east dotted with large trees on the horizon is the ancient Baal-Hazor (2 Sam. 13 : 23). This region is the country of Gideon, the valiant judge who rose up and delivered the Israelites out of the hands of the Midianites and Amalekites, when they "lay along the valley like grasshoppers for multitude" (Judge. 7 : 12).

Descending the gradient we enter a broad, fertile valley in which lies the picturesquely located village of Jifna, ancient Gophna. On the hill to the left is Bir-Zeit — Berzetho of Josephus. This is also where Judas Maccabeus fell, battling against Bacchides. Down in the valley is the village of Ein-Sinia and above, on the right, is seen the ruined Crusader castle of Baldwin (Arabic: Qasr Bardawill). In the picturesque valley flanked with rugged cliffs ahead are the "springs of the robbers" — as called in Arabic Ayoun El Haramiyeh.

From here the road begins to follow the ascent and soon we arrive at a broad, cultivated plain on the east called the Plain of the Maidens through which a road leads to Seilun — which marks the site of the important ancient town and sanctuary of SHILOH. The Biblical SHILOH was a place of considerable importance. It was the home of the Ark of The Covenant (1 Sam. 4 : 3), here the maidens danced at the annual festival in honour of the Lord. On one of those occasions the Benjaminites (who had been refused wives from the community) raided the festival and abucted the maidens. (Judg. 21 : 19—21). A Danish expedition explored the region and made considerable diggings on the site between 1929-32 and discovered traces of Canaanite, Hebrew and Byzantine occupations.

The modern road from Jerusalem to Nablus (Shechem) follows the old one, as described in Judges 21:19 — **Then they said, Behold, there is a feast of the Lord in Shiloh yearly, in a place which is on the north side of Bethel, on the south side of Lebonah.**

Old olive trees

The plain of Lebonah — a view from the hill
The steep descent of the main road leading north from Jerusalem to Nablus (Shechem) is seen on the left. The village of Lubban, the Biblical Lebonah, standing on the slope of the far hill across the plain, is on the right.

A short distance from Shiloh, from the top of a hill overlooking the charming view of a small plain, the village of Lubban which has faithfully preserved its Biblical name of Lebonah, can be seen. Descending, the road crosses the plain and leads north past the villages of Kuza and Howwara. Close by is the village of Awarta, where the tombs of the High Priest Elazar, son of Aaron, and his son Phinehas are shown (Josh. 24:33). The road goes now through the great plain of Mukhnah and arrives at the large Arab town of Nablus (Shechem), situated between Mt. Gerizim and Mt. Ebal.

At the base of Mt. Gerizim is Jacob's Well where Jesus spoke to the Samaritan woman of Sychar (John 4 : 5—42). The present village of Askar is identical with Sychar. The great importance and interest of the well from every point of view can hardly be emphasized; it is undoubtedly the very well claimed by the ancients to have been dug by the Patriarch Jacob (Gen. 33 : 19). The well is about 105 feet deep and its water is good. The property belongs to the Greek Orthodox church who has built over the well a large and still unfinished church. This stands on the foundations of a Crusader church. Even in the 4th century a Christian church enclosed the well.

We continue northwest past the village of Ballata where ancient **Shechem** was situated. Excavations at Ballata were initiated by Prof. Selin

Jacob's Well in Sychar (Shechem — Nablus)

Uncompleted church standing on the foundations of a Crusader church (above). Greek Orthodox priest in the garden near the church (below-left). The well's shaft (below-right) is cylindrical and lined with masonry, 105 feet deep and about 9 feet in diameter. Its top is a large, pierced stone — itself obviously of great age.

The town of Nablus — Shechem

in 1914 and continued in subsequent years. Massive constructions were unearthed proving the city to have been established in the middle bronze age (about 2000 B.C.) and to have flourished through later ages. Just outside Nablus (Shechem) was the scene of Joshua's convening of Israel where the Blessings and Cursings — prescribed by Moses — were pronounced to the assembled Tribes from Mt. Gerizim and Mt. Ebal respectively (Josh. 24:1-25, 8:30-35). Shechem was the scene of the ruse and massacre carried out by the sons of Jacob upon Shechemites and their ruler in revenge for the ravishing of their sister Dinah by the king's son. Until the reign of Omri Shechem was the capital of the Northern Kingdom of Israel, but when the seat of the government was transfered to the newly founded city of Samaria, not far distant, Shechem lost its importance and dwindled.

In the Acts (7 : 16) the town is referred to as Sychem. In 67 A.D. Vespasian slew 11,000 of its inhabitants and destroyed the town. After the termination of the Jewish war the Emperor Titus rebuilt and renamed it Flavia Neapolis. From this name we have the modern Nablus. Nablus is a city of about 45.000 inhabitants, mostly Moslem Arabs, situated between Mt. Gerizim and Mt. Ebal.

Samaritans at prayer

Samaritan Priest with old "Torah" Scroll

THE SAMARITANS. A singular feature of Nablus is the survival in it of practically the sole remnant of the very ancient race of Samaritans — the original inhabitants of the city. An interesting little community, numbering today 250 people, preserving in their religious services and practices many ancient customs. Their written language is the Samaritan which is similar to the ancient Hebrew, but having a number of different characters differently formed. The High Priest presides over their religious services and is also the head of the community.

Nablus was occupied by the Arabs in 636. Some of its present mosques were originally Byzantine or Crusader churches.

Leaving Nablus, we continue north-

Samaria-Sebaste — Roman ruins

east and come in about 15—20 minutes drive to the village of Sebastieh built on the slope of a hill where Samaria stood.

Samaria was founded by Omri, king of Israel in 876 B.C. (1 Kings 16 : 24). He purchased the hill from one, Shemer and it is probable that the name of the city — Shomeron in Hebrew — takes its origin from the former owner. The city became the new capital of Israel and the residence of Ahab and subsequent kings of the Northern kingdom. In the year 721 B.C. Samaria was conquered and burnt by Sargon, the Assyrian — king of Ninveh. Those who survived the destruction were, except for a few of the lower classes, carried off into captivity and were replaced by immigrants from Mesopotamia brought in by the conqueror to replace them. These newcomers were later called Samaritans. The destruction of Samaria marked the extinction of the Kingdom of Israel and henceforth Judah was to stand alone. Alexander the Great captured the town in 331 B.C. John Hyrcanus destroyed it again in 129 B.C. Herod the Great restored the town and fortified it in 27 B.C. and added many fine buildings. He renamed it SEBASTE (in honour of his patron — Augustus) from Sebastos, the Greek parallel of Augustus. The Acts of the Apostles speaks of the Apostles Peter and John, and of Philip the Deacon preaching and ministering "in the cities of Samaria".

Samaria-Sebaste — ruins of Omri-Ahab palace

Samaria — Sebaste — Roman theatre and Israelite wall

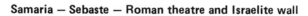

Samaria-Sebaste — Colonnaded street — main entrance to the town

Watchtower in a vineyard in Samaria

SAMARIA—SHOMERON

THE DISTRICT OF SAMARIA was in the Biblical period the geographical center of Palestine. It was one of the three sections of the hill country which runs like a rocky spine from Syria, through Galilee and Judea to the Negev desert in the south. Its name is believed to come from "Shomeron" (Hebrew: "Place of Watch"). In the inheritance of Canaan by the Israelites much of what became Samaria was allotted to the Tribe of Ephraim and Half-Tribe of Manasseh. Samaria was the main portion of what was known after Solomon's time as the Northern Kingdom in contrast to Judah. It reached from the Mediterranean to the Jordan and extended south from the mountain mass of Gilboa and Mt. Ephraim and the south-east, north-west ridge of Carmel. From the narrow pass at Megiddo a network of ancient roads ran in every direction, giving the people of Samaria contact with many other nations. Samaria, far better supplied with natural resources than Judea, led Isaiah to call it "the head of Ephraim" (7:9), and to immortalize its "glorious beauty, which is on the head of the fat valley". Throughout their history Samaria and Judea were rivals rather than neighbours. The two were united by King David (c. 1000—960 B.C.) and remained in the united kingdom of Solomon (c. 960—922 B.C.). But at Solomon's death the units were again separated, with Rehoboam succeeding to the throne of Judah in the south and Jeroboam taking the Ten Tribes which formed the Northern Kingdom.

IMPORTANT TOWNS IN SAMARIA were — Tirzah, where early kings were crowned (1 Kings 16:15, 23), Samaria (Shomeron-Sebaste) founded by King Omri as his capital (c. 876—869 B.C.), Shechem (Nablus today) (Its role was important in Israel's history for it was situated in the pivotal pass between Mt. Ebal and Mt. Gerizim and dominated roads north and west. After the destruction of the Samaritan temple on Mt. Gerizim, Vespasian rebuilt here his new city — "Neapolis"), Shiloh (an important sanctuary town) — resting place of the Ark of The Covenant. To this place Joshua brought the Tribes of Israel at the close of the main phase of their conquest), Megiddo (Armageddon), Taanach, Ein-Ganim (Jenin) and Hazor. Before the Six Day War in 1967 the frontier of Jordan, near the town of Tul-Karm formed a great bulge and Israel at that area (see Nathanya) was only about 14 miles wide. For about 18 years since the Ceasefire in 1949 Jordanian sentries sat on the hills in the east, gazing straight across Israel, at the shipping on the Mediterranean. The main road from Jerusalem to Megiddo, through Mt. Ephraim and Samaria, passes through a most interesting and picturesque countryside, so rich in Biblical and Israel's history. In a land where great agricultural changes have occurred in the last 30—40 years, this countryside is perhaps the finest surviving stretch of old Palestine.

In Israel, the tractor, irrigation and scientific agriculture have transformed a once barren land into fruitful country and even the stones have disappeared. But ancient habits and customs have also vanished, and only in Samaria may one still see the Biblical life of other days preserved by Arab peasants, who replaced or continued the conservatism of the Canaanites and Israelites.

Harvest time in Samaria

Samaria — ploughing the field

The main road continues north, passes by an arched aqueduct that crosses the valley and ascends the hill. Halting at the top, we have before us a delightful panorama of the country, embracing Mts. Hermon and Carmel, and the Mediterranean coastline; and looking back, a good view of Samaria.

At about mile 60 the road runs quite close to the mound ("Tell") DOTHAN where Joseph was let down by his brethren into the pit and where they sold him to the Ishmaelite traders who took him to Egypt (Gen. 37:17-28).

Crossing the fertile, nicely cultivated Plain of Dothan, we soon enter the town of Jenin which stands on the edge of the great plain of Esdraelon (Jezreel Valley). Jenin is ancient EN-GANIM (Spring of gardens) of Josh. 19:21. Tradition associates the town with Jesus' curing of the ten lepers. (Luke 17:11—19). Two roads lead from Jenin to the Valley of Jezreel-Esdraelon, both crossing the pre-1967 border between Jordan and Israel. One road, to the left, goes

north and leads to Megiddo-Armageddon, Mt. Carmel and Haifa. The other goes straight, east, passes by the ruins of the town of Jezreel where King Ahab and Queen Jezebel had a palace, and where they robbed poor Naboth of his vineyard (1 Kings 21.1). Beyond Jezreel, on the right, are seen the mountains of Gilboa on which King Saul fought his last and disastrous battle against the Philistines and where he and his son Jonathan were killed and by which was closed the first chapter of the Israelite Monarchy, to usher in the brilliant period of David's reign. In his lament over Saul and Jonathan, his dear friend, David cried out: "The beauty of Israel is slain upon the high places; how are the mighty fallen"... (2 Sam. 1:17—21).

The road continues through the Valley of Jezreel-Esdraelon, one of the most celebrated battlefields of the ancient world, — a vast, well-watered, exceedingly fertile plain known as the "bread-basket" of Israel. The town of Afula, in the center of the valley was founded in 1925, when the plain was mostly swamps and a malaria stricken area.

Several road lead from Afula in all directions: One goes west, past Megiddo-Armageddon, and via the Eeron pass comes to the Mediterranean; the second leads south-east, passes by the springs of Harod where Gideon mustered his men in a pitched camp before his pursuit of the Midianites (Judg. 7); it continues along the Gilboa mountains and comes to the old town of Beth-She'an.

The Jezreel-Esdraelon Valley

Mount Tabor

The Afula-Tiberias main road continues in a north-easterly direction past the village of Nain, scene of the raising of the widow's son by Jesus (Luke 7: 11-15). Nearby, also on the right, is the site of En-Dor, reminiscent of the story of the witch of Endor, whom Saul consulted on the eve of his fatal battle of Gilboa (I Sam. 28:7-25).

A Road Inn operated by members of Kibbutz Daverat is on the left side of the road. Proceeding past Mt. Tabor, the highway goes through Kefar-Tavor (a road from here leads to Yavneel and Kinneret) and arrives at the "Golani Junction" where it joins with the Nazareth—Tiberias road (see page 131).

TABOR is one of the finest mountains of Gaililee possessing a definite beauty, rising, as it does to great height abruptly out of the surrounding plain (about 1850 feet above sea level — 1650 feet above the valley). The Old Testament knows Mt. Tabor as a fortified retreat of the Northern Tribes. From this region Deborah and Barak, son of Abinoam recruited their forces to advance against Sisera, captain of the army of Jabin the Canaanite, king of Hazor (Judg. 4:6, 5:15). Mount Tabor was generally accepted as the scene of the **Transfiguration** of Jesus, and was so considered as early as the 3rd century. In the Gospel account of the Transfiguration, the name of the mountain is not given (Luke 9:28); but St. Luke says, after the account of Christ's discourse at Caesarea Philippi: *"And it came to pass about in eight days after these sayings, he took Peter and John and James, and went up to a mountain to pray"*. The journey could easily have been made to Tabor in this interval; however, many would look to Mt. Hermon as being the more likely place, — chiefly, no doubt, because it lies so close to Caesarea Philippi.

St. Luke continues: *"And as he prayed, the fashion of his countenance was altered and his raiment was white and glistering. And behold, there talked with him two men, which were Moses and Elijah; who appeared in glory, and spake of his decease which he should accomplish in Jerusalem"*.

127

Church building at Nain — view of Mt. Tabor

ASCENT AND VISIT TO MT. TA-
BOR. A road branches off the highway and leads to the top of the mount
through the village of Dabbouryeh.
Small cars only (no buses) can travel
on these steep and hairpin curves.
Arriving at the plateau the road
divides; the left branch leads to the
Greek, and the other to the Latin
property. Just before the fork a
fragment of the wall of Josephus is
noticed, erected by the historian of
the Jewish War (65 A.D.) when he was
still in command of the revolutionary
forces in Galilee. The road to the right
goes through a large medieval gate and
comes to the magnificent new Basilica
of the Transfiguration, which was
completed and consecrated in 1924. It
is in the style of the Christian architecture of the 4th and 5th centuries,
the beauty of which readily strikes
one; it combines the Eastern and
Western styles with a happy blending.

The facade is divided into two stories,
with a very flamboyant looking entrance, which consists of a large
rectangular door set in from the
vestibule. The latter is covered with a
very large and richly sculptured
Byzantine arch, surrounded by a ga-
ble. The church is built over the
remains of earlier sanctuaries — one
built by the Benedictines in the 13th
century, which in its turn stood upon
the ruins of an earlier chapel. The
ancient construction has been care-
fully preserved and may be seen
incorporated into the new.

THE INTERIOR is divided into three
naves by pillars; the central nave is
higher than the aisles and terminates
in a beautiful, semicircular apse pierced by windows. The central apse
contains a lovely mosaic representa-
tion of the Transfiguration.

From the centre of the church a large
flight of steps decends to the crypt in

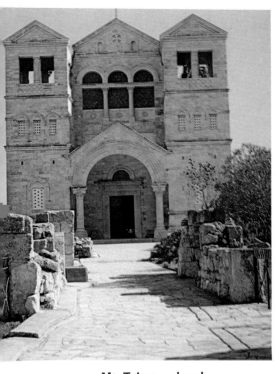

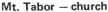

Mt. Tabor — church

Mt. Tabor — church (interior)

which the ancient walls and altar — revealed by excavations — are preserved. The crypt is adorned with representations of the Trinity. The lateral naves and chapels are dedicated to the Holy Sacraments and the Immaculate Conception. The chapels to the right and left of the entrance are dedicated to Moses and Elijah. The Franciscans have, besides the Basilica, a large monastery and a hospice for pilgrims. The view from Tabor is superb! The mount is covered with a variety of shrubs and trees, including the oak and terebinth. The top is a big tableland 1300 meters long and 450 wide (1 meter = 3.3 feet). Tabor, like Carmel and Hermon, is often mentioned in a poetic and metaphorical sense in the Old Testament. Jeremiah, prophesying Nebuchadnessar's invasion says, "He shall come like Tabor among the mountains, like Carmel above the sea".

Returning to the highway and the town of Afula, the road to Nazareth leads north through the Jezreel-Esdraelon Valley. Ascending the hill, seen on the right is an abrupt and rocky cliff with a sheer drop into the valley. This prominent hill lies just south of Nazareth and is called the Hill of Precipitation (Luke 4:28—30). From the top of the west rim of the 1,600 feet high basin may be seen a 30-mile panorama unfolding in three directions, and rich in Old Testament history. On the east the Jordan Valley wall and the long range of Gilead rim the horizon. To the south lies the Plain of Jezreel Esdraelon with its scores of battlefields identified with Israel's struggles, topped by mountains and the mounds of Beth-She'an, Tabor, Gilboa and Megiddo. To the west runs the storied Carmel ridge as it plunges into the blue Mediterranean.

129

The town of Nazareth

NAZARETH, about 1,250 feet above sea level, a very pleasantly situated town, scattered loosely over the terraces of the hills and in the valleys between them, was the home of Jesus, were He spent His childhood and early youth and where He worked in the trade of a carpenter. Nazareth possesses a good and copious fountain in the center of town called the Spring of Our Lady Mary. Near it is the Greek Orthodox church of St. Gabriel, also called the church of The Annunciation. The new Franciscan Basilica of The Annunciation was rebuilt a few years ago over the church that stood here since 1730 — on the site of a church of the Middle Ages. This sanctuary is believed to mark the house of Joseph and Mary and it covers a natural grotto believed to have been their dwelling.

A few hundred feet to the northeast stands the church of St. Joseph, known as the "Workshop of Joseph" and a short distance from here is the Greek Catholic church connected with a hall considered to have been the synagogue of Nazareth in the time of Christ, in which He taught and read from the Scroll (Luke 4:14—31).

Nazareth was the residence of Joseph and Mary (Luke 1:26) whence they journeyed 85 miles south to Bethlehem for the Roman Enrollment (Luke 2:4).

A new part of Nazareth called "Nazareth-Illit", settled mostly by new immigrants, was built on the hilltop east of the town.

Proceeding east, the road passes on the left the village of Mash'had, site of the Biblical Gath-Hefer, birthplace of the prophet Jonah and descends to Kafr-Kanna — CANA of Galilee, scene of Christ's first miracle — turning water into wine at the marriage feast (John 2:1—11).

Cana of Galilee — general view

Cana — Church

Beyond Cana is the little valley and village of Tur'an. The road continues to the "Golani Junction" with its War Memorial (War of Independence—1948), where it joins with the Afula-Mt. Tabor road. A few minutes drive from here, on the hill, off the main road, is Kibbutz Lavi with its nice, well-run and inviting Guest House. We now enter the volcanic zone of Lower

Kibbutz Lavi — Guest House

Galilee. On the left is an elongated rocky hill resembling a saddle called Horns of Hattin. Here was fought the great battle on July 4th.1187, in which the Crusaders suffered a crushing defeat at the hands of Saladin, which brought to an end the Latin Kingdom of Jerusalem and ended Christian rule in the greater part of the country.

The beautiful blue expanse of the Sea of Galilee suddenly breaks into view with the town of Tiberias on its shore and the slope of the hill. Opposite, across the lake in the east are the Golan Heights (in Syria before the Six Day War in 1967). The town of Zefat (Safed) and the high mountains of Upper Galilee are seen above on our left, and in the far distant northeast Mt. Hermon raises its towering mass.

TIBERIAS, capital of Lower Galilee, was built by Herod Antipas in 21 A.D. who named it in honour of the Emperor Tiberius. It lies on the west shore of the Sea of Galilee (Lake Kinneret, or Lake Tiberias) about 12 miles south west of the entrance of the Jordan into the lake and about 6 miles north of the river's exit in the south.

After the fall and destruction of Jerusalem in 70 A.D., following the Great Jewish Revolt, Tiberias became an important Jewish metropolis and center of Rabbinic learning; by the 2nd century it was recognized, with Jerusalem, Hebron and Zefat (Safed) as one of the four sacred cities of

131

Tiberias and the Sea of Galilee

the Holyland, the seat of the Great Sanhedrin which moved here from Sepphoris. The Jewish codes and traditional laws known as the Mishna, were compiled here in 200 A.D. and in the 4th century the famous Talmudic School of Tiberias completed the Jerusalem Talmud. Many famous Rabbis and scholars lived and studied, died and were buried in Tiberias; the illustrious Harambam (Maimonides), the Jewish philosopher and writer of the 12th century whose tomb is in the center of town, Rabbi Meir Baal-Hanes, Rabbi Akiva, Rabbi Yohanan Ben-Zakai, Rabbi Hiyya and others — all famous for their religious teachings.

Tiberias was taken by the Arabs in 637 A.D. It was occupied by the Crusaders in 1099. It fell to Saladin as a result of the Battle of Hattin in 1187. In 1242 the town was again captured by an Egyptian Sultan. In 1560 Suleiman the Magnificent, the Turkish Sultan, bestowed Tiberias upon the Jew Don Joseph Nasi; when it received many Jewish settlers. In the 18th century the town revived under the administration of Sheikh Daher Al Omar, who restored its walls and castle. In 1837 it was demolished, in great part, by an earthquake and on Sept. 20, 1918 it was taken by the British General Allenby. Tiberias lies about 700 feet below sea level, its climate is excellent in winter and it is a most popular resort with many beautiful hotels. The Hot Springs and Baths on the coast south of the town are well known for their healing properties. The ancient town of Hamath stood here near the hot springs, which were much patronized in the Roman period. Excavations have brought to light a synagogue and remains of Roman buildings.

Tiberias — old city wall

In the 18th century Tiberias revived under the progressive administration of Sheikh Daher al'Omar, who restored its walls and castle, in 1738. The walls were restored again by Ibrahim Pasha, in 1833, only to be demoslished, in great part, by the earthquake four years later, which also shattered many buildings of the town.

Details from the mosaic floor of the 2nd-3rd century synagogue of Hammata, the town which occupied the site of biblical Hammath in Naphtali (Josh. 19:35).

133

Peacock, symbol of immortality — detail from the mosaic floor of
the 4th century church at Tabgha.

THE SEA OF GALILEE is 14 miles long (north to south) and about 7 miles at its widest point. It was in this beautiful region that much of the Gospel story was enacted, and these are the waters when raging tempestously in a storm, subsided, as we read in St. Matthew's Gospel (8 : 26) at Chirst's command. On this shore He taught the multitudes, fed the thousands, and healed the sick ; upon these waves Jesus walked and met His disciples when they had toiled vainly all night against the fury of the storm (Matt. 14 : 22—23).

FROM TIBERIAS, VIA GINNOSAR TO TABGAH AND CAPERNAUM

The road leading north from Tiberias to Capernaum goes along the shore of the Sea of Galilee. It passes by the remains of Magdala — home of Mary Magdalene (Luke 8:2) and enters the Plain of Gennesaret. The beautiful, welcoming Guest House of Nof Ginossar is on the shore of the Sea of Galilee, off the main road, on the right. Ascending the hill and turning off to the right, the road comes to Tabgha with its most beautiful mosaic floor at the 4th century church of the Multiplication of the Loaves and Fishes. The mosaic floor depicts the water birds and flora of this region and symbols of the five loaves and two fishes (Matt. 14:14—21). Near here are the "Seven Springs" of Ein Tabgha (Greek:Heptapegon). Above, on the left is the Mount of Beatitudes — scene of the Sermon on the Mount with its beautiful small chapel.

"Nof Ginossar" — Guest House

Tabgha — The Loaves and Fishes — mosaic floor at the church

Tabgha — 4th century church with beautiful mosaic floor

The Mount of Beatitudes — church

The road continues eastward a short distance along the shore and ends at the enclosed property of the Franciscans in which stand the synagogue ruins of **Capernaum.** A busy little lake port on the north shore of the Sea of Galilee, not far from the entrance of the Jordan to the lake, Capernaum was a center for Jesus' busy Galilean ministry. Rather than Nazareth, it was called "His own city" (Matt. 9:1). Capernaum was apparently a Roman military post along a highway from Damascus to Galilee and south to Jerusalem — a road from whose tax-collector's booth Jesus called Matthew (Levi) to discipleship (Matt. 9:9). He also taught on the plain from a boat, or in a Capernaum synagogue (Mark 1:21) — possibly that erected by the centurion (Luke 7:5) (Other references — Matt. 11:23; Mark 3:3—11; John 4:46—54).

To excavators Capernaum has yielded ruins of one of the most elegant white lime-stone synagogues in Israel, now partly restored, and dating back from the 3rd—4th century A.D. Like other synagogues, it faced Jerusalem; its main portion was a rectangular, columned basilica. It had a main and two side entrances, was paved with limestones, many of which are still visible, and had two rows of stone benches, one above the other, running around three sides. A gallery used by women ran around the north-west and east sides.

A short distance from here, on the hill, are the ruins of **Chorazin.** The village of **Bethsaida,** "The House of Fishermen" lay in this region, near the Jordan. It was the home of the Disciples Peter, Andrew and Philip. Beyond this, on the east side of the Sea of Galilee was the "Country of the Gadarenes, which was over against Galilee", where Jesus cast out the unclean spirit from a man possessed, and where He permitted the devils to enter the herd of swine (Luke 8:26-33).

Capernaum — old synagogue ruins

A new road from Capernaum leads east, across the (upper) Jordan over "Arik" Bridge and follows the eastern shore of the Sea of Galilee. It passes by the excavated site of Kursi and comes to Kibbutz Ein-Gev. A short distance from "Arik" Bridge, a road to the left ascends the hill and connects with the main road leading to Kuneitra on the Golan Heights.

Capernaum synagogue — a restoration

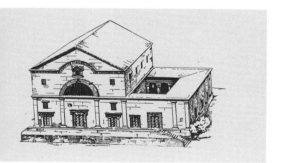

Tabgha — church

Capernaum and the Sea of Galilee

CAPERNAUM —
GENERAL VIEW OF
EXCAVATED AREA

The synagogue of
Capernaum of the
third-fourth
century A.D.

Ruins of houses
in use from 1st
cent. B.C. until
about 5th cent. A.D

Fifth cent. church
built upon the
traditional house
of St. Peter

Column's head with "Menorah"

Column's head with an urn and a cluster of grapes

CAPERNAUM EXCAVATIONS

Baker's millstone

House of St. Peter

Ruins of the synagogue —
Greek-Orthodox church in background

Entrance to the site

Sea of Galilee fish ("St. Peter's") — Fresh-water Bass

The famous **Tiberias Hot Springs** are about 1½ miles south of the town. Remains of the Roman Spa and a beautiful, most interesting mosaic floor of the old synagogue of Hammath are near the modern bathhouses. The road follows the shore of the lake and comes to one of the famous pioneering settlements in the country — **Kinneret**. Its cemetery, on a little hill near the lake's shore, is a resting place for many of its founders. The national poetess, **Rachel**, who was a member of Kinneret is also buried here. A short distance from here, off the road to the left, are the ruins of **Beit-Yerah**, the "city of the moon" which was a center of early civilization in the country (Middle Bronze Age) and survived as Philoteria into the Byzantine era.

Kibbutz Deganya, the first communal settlement in the country, is near the southern end of the Sea of Galilee, where the coast opens again, marking the beginning of the Jordan Valley. Pouring out of the lake like a stream the **Jordan River** cuts its way through the valley, first due west, and then striking south along the base of the hills until it reaches the Dead Sea in which it loses itself completely (a distance of 65 miles as the crow flies, falling 590 feet, or an average of 9 feet a mile). History has magnified the Jordan in the thinking of reverent or merely interested millions out of all proportions to its actual size. To be sure, its basic importance can not be magnified, because its role in history has been great beyond all rational measurement.

The Jordan River at its exist from the Sea of Galilee near Degania

JORDAN, BETH-SHE'AN AND JEZREEL VALLEYS.

From Deganya the road follows the shore of the Sea of Galilee via Kibbutz Ma'agan and past Tel-Katzir to Kibbutz Ein-Gev, on the eastern bank. where a very nice fish restaurant and Gift-Shop are operated by members of the settlement. (A detour southeast leads to Gadara). Another road branches off and leads south through the Jordan Valley. Just after passing Kibbutz Gesher a road leads right, ascends the steep hill and comes to the remains of the Crusader fortress of Belvoir overlooking a magnificent and breathtaking view of the Jordan Valley, the Gilead mountains and the Sea of Galilee. It was built in the 12th cen-

tury by the Knights of the Order of Hospitallers. It was the scene of fierce battles between the Crusaders and Saracens until it surrendered in 1189.

Continuing through the Jordan Valley past Kibbutz Gesher, the road comes to the old city of Beth-She'an (Shan), one of the oldest occupied sites in the country, with the first of its explored 18-level mound dating back more than 5000 years. King Saul and his three sons, including Johathan, were killed at nearby Mt. Gilboa and their bodies were fastened to the city wall of Beth-She'an (1 Sam. 31: Chron. 10). In new Testament times Beth-She'an was known as Scythopolis and was one of the largest of the chain of ten Greek cities — the Decapolis.

The settlement of Kinneret in the Jordan Valley near the southern shore of the Sea of Galilee, the Jordan River, and the Golan Heights

"BIK'AH" (valley) ROAD TO JERUSALEM.

A newly opened road, constructed after 1967 leads south from Beth-She'an, along the west bank of the Jordan River to Jericho, the Dead Sea and Jerusalem — the river itself is the present border. It passes by the new settlements of Mehola, Argaman, Masua, Phasael and Gilgal.

BETH-SHE'AN TO AFULA.

Another road from Beth-She'an leads west to the Jezreel Valley, along the mountain range of Gilboa and past the "Sachnah" (Gan Hashlosha) springs. This road passes very close to Kibbutz Beth-Alfa-Heftzi-Bah. Most interesting remains of a Jewish synagogue of the 6th century were discovered here. They were subsequently excavated and revealed a fine mosaic floor with elaborate Biblical and other representations including the Ark of the Covenant, Abraham's Sacrifice, the signs of the Zodiac. the seasons, etc.

A few miles before reaching Afula a road leads left to the Well of Harod, also called Gideon's Fountain. Here Gideon encamped with his army before the battle against the Midianites and here he put his men to the test at this brook; those who knelt down and drank right out of the stream being rejected, (Judg. 7:1—7). Near Kibbutz Ein-Harod a road turns right and leads to Belvoir Crusader Fortress.

Jordan river's exit from the Sea of Galilee

FROM KINNERET TO MT. TABOR.

The road ascends the steep hill over-looking the green and beautiful Jordan Valley with its many pioneering settlements, with the mountains of Golan and Gilead in the east. The road continues west through the valley and village of Yavne'el and comes to Mt. Tabor—at the juncture of the territory of Issachar (Josh. 19:22) Zebulun and Naphtali.

UPPER GALILEE AND GOLAN HEIGHTS.

The road from Tiberias and Lower Galilee leads north, past Capernaum, ascends the hills and comes to Rosh-Pina — the oldest Jewish Colony in Upper Galilee, established in 1882. From here a road ascends the mountain and reaches Zefat (Safed) capi-tal of Upper Galilee, about 2800 feet above sea level. Zefat is an old city and one of the four sacred cities in the country (the first being Jerusalem and the other two are Tiberias and Hebron). It is probably the Zef, of Josephus, which he himself fortified against the Romans, Saphet of the Crusaders, which they fortified. Under the Moslems Safed was the capital of the Northern district. It gained fame in the 16th century when a group of Cabbalists

Zefat — The Holy Ark at the old synagogue of the "Ari"

Zefat (Safed) — general view

"Hazafon" Hotel — Kiryat Shmona

Hazor — ruins

neaded by Rabbi Itzhak Lourie settled in the town, which since then became known as the "city of the mystic studies of the Cabbala".

Zefat-Safed is a popular summer resort with many nice hotels and an interesting Artists Colony.

From Rosh Pina the road continues north, through the Huleh Valley — formerly swamps, marshes and mala- ria stricken area, now reclaimed and developed. It passes near the mound and excavated remains of Biblical Hazor, a key city mentioned in the account of the Israelite occupation of Canaan. Hazor was the chief city of Jabin, chief of the confederacy and king of Canaan, (Josh. 11:1—14). Barak defeated Sisera, the general of Jabin of Hazor (Judg. 4:17, 1 Kings

Kibbutz Ayelet-Hashahar — Guest House

Kefar-Giladi — Guest House

9:15). Nearby, on the right is Kibbutz Ayelet Hashahar ("Morning Star") with its famous, most beautiful and inviting Guest House.

The main road continues north and leads to the large town of Kiryat-Shmonah. **The first turning** to the right leads to Yesud Hama'ala, to Kibbutz Hulata and to the Huleh Natural Reserve. **The second turning,** to the left, leads to Metzudat Koah (Nabi Yosha) and the Northern Frontier road (Kedesh Naphtali, Malkiyeh, Yir'on, Avivim, Bar'am, Dovev, Sa'sa, and/or to Yiftah, Ramim-Manara, Margaliot and Kfar-Giladi-Tel-Hai). **The third turning** (right) leads to Kibbutz Kfar Blum with its lovely, well-run Guest House (also to Gonen and other settlements in the area).

The main road continues north to Tel-Hai with its famous lion monument for the Galilean hero, Joseph Trumpeldor and his friends. The large old building of Tel-Hai serves today as a museum and a memorial to the brave early pioneer settlers in this part of the country. A short distance from here is the very early pioneering settlement (Kibbutz) of Kfar-Giladi, with its nice and friendly Guest House. The little, northernmost village in Israel, Metula, with its famous "Good Fence", is about 4 miles further north, right on the border of Lebanon.

Tel-Hai — Tomb of Joseph Trumpeldor

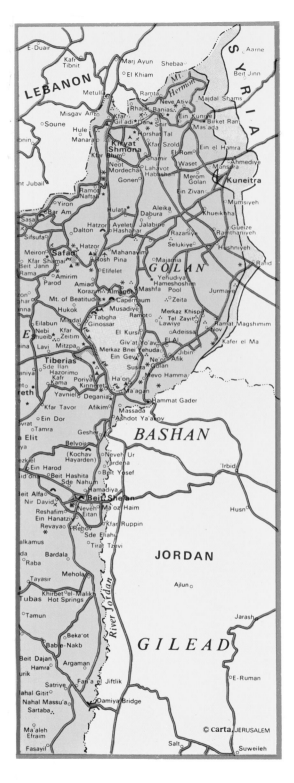

At the town of Kiryat-Shmonah we turn east, drive by Kibbutz Hagoshrim (Guest House) and passing Kibbutz Daphna and Dan arrive at the former, pre-1967 border with Syria. The sources and main tributaries of the Jordan River are in this area at the base of snow covered (most of the year) Mt. Hermon. Nearby and well-worth visiting is the recently excavated Tel Dan, ("Dan to Beer-Sheva" — Dan-Laish, Judg. 18:12-14). Close by also is the beautiful and interesting Dan Natural Reserve. A most interesting museum of Natural History is open for visits at Kibbutz Dan.

Ascending the Golan (Heights) mountain range the road reaches the springs of Banias — site of Caesarea Philippi, "A Gentile City" at the southern base of Mt. Hermon. Constructed by Philip, son of Herod the Great (4 B.C. — 34 A.D.), named in honour of Philip's Caesar, Emperor Tiberius; its site (Paneas) has long been a favourite seat of the Greek and Roman nature cult god Pan and of Canaanite fertility deities, worshipped in a cave from which issued a main source of the Jordan River. Matthew (16:13) and Mark (8:27) both mention Caesarea Philippi as the scene of Peter's great confession of Jesus as "The Christ..." This may be near the scene of the Transfiguration (Matt. 17), (See Mt. Tabor).

The road ascends the heights, past many former Syrian "Bunkers" and fortifications from which, between 1948 and 1967, the Syrians troubled

and shot at the Israeli settlements in the low-lying Huleh Valley. A newly built road branches off to the left and leads up to the remains of the 12th century Crusader fortress of ("Kal'at") Nimrod. Continuing straight, the steep, winding road comes to the Druze village of Mas'adeh, from where, turning left, it goes to "Birket Ram" — a large natural water reservoir — and via another Druze village, Majdel-Shams, it ascends the snow slopes of Mt. Hermon.

Turning right at Mas'adeh, the road leads south through the high plateau past the Druze village of Bouk'ata and the new settlement of El-rom. From here, a road leads west via the ruined former Syrian base of Wasset and descends to Kibbutz Gonen in the Huleh Valley. Proceeding straight on the plateau, the road arrives at the outskirts of Kuneitra, which, following negotiations after the "Yom Kippur" War in 1973, was handed back to Syria by Israel. Small detachments of U.N. troops are stationed here between the Israeli and Syrian positions near the cease-fire line. The main road to the Syrian capital of Damascus leads east from Kuneitra.

Straight to the south, the road continues on the plateau, descending near El-Hamma (Hammat-Gader — Gadara) to the Jordan Valley. Near the new settlement of El-Al a new road descends to Kibbutz Ein-Gev, on the eastern bank of the Sea of Galilee.

Turning right near Kuneitra, the road passes by Ein-Zivan, descends westwards via Nafah and comes to the destroyed, former heavily fortified Syrian "Bunkers" on the "Murtafa" hill overlooking Kibbutz Gadot across the pre-1967 border. Crossing the (upper) Jordan over "Jacob's Daughters Bridge", the main road continues via Mahanaim to Rosh-Pinna.

The Banias Springs

Israeli and U.N. soldiers near Kuneitra

Monument for fallen Israeli soldiers

Former Syrian "Bunkers"

Snow-covered Mount Hermon

The sources — tributaries of the Jordan River near Mt. Hermon

FROM JERUSALEM TO HAIFA

Jerusalem highway — burnt trucks

2. THROUGH THE SHARON VALLEY TO MEGIDDO, HAIFA & CAESAREA

The main road from Jerusalem to Tel-Aviv-Jaffa leads north-west through the mountains of Judea. The border between Jordan and Israel before the Six Day War in 1967 was across the deep gorge on the right. The tower-crowned hill on the horizon ahead is **Mizpah** ("Nabi Samwil"). The Jewish National Fund has planted millions of trees — Pine, Eucalyptus and Cypress — on all the hills, as far as the eye can see. **Kirjat-Jearim** ("city of forests"), a Gibeonite town (Josh. 9:17) occupied by the Tribe of Dan (Judg. 18:12) was a short distance from Jerusalem. In this frontier town of Judah and Benjamin the Ark of the Covenant rested before David conveyed it to Jerusalem (1 Sam. 6:21, 7:1; 2 Sam. 6:2). It was the home of the prophet Urijah (Jerm. 26:20). Many identify it with the present day Abu-Ghosh, a little hill village c. 7 miles from Jerusalem on the road to Jaffa. Abu-Ghosh contains remnants of an elegant Crusader church. Closeby are the farming settlements of **Kiryat-Anavim** and **Ma'aleh-Ha'chamisha**, well known for their mountain resort Guest Houses.

From the top of the hill ahead, before descending through a narrow valley, the first glimpse of the Mediterranean is obtained. The burnt trucks seen here along the road were left as monuments to the brave drivers and truck crews who were killed during the 1948 War of Independence, when help was being rushed to the besieged city of Jerusalem. Reaching the plain near the abandoned Inn at **Bab El Wad**, the road straight ahead, which is open to small vehicles only, leads via Latroun and through the **Valley of Ajalon** where Joshua commanded the sun to stand still...(Josh. 10:12-13). Turning left (for buses and heavy vehicles), the pre-1967 road leads to Beth-Shemesh from where it continues straight via the Valley of Elah to the Lachish Region and Ashkelon (see Jerusalem-Ashkelon route). Past "Samson's Inn" — a Road Inn and Gas station close to Zorah and Eshtaol where Samson was born — the main highway leads to the town of Ramlah. At mile 21, a whitish hill on the right was the **Biblical Gezer** (Josh. 16:10).

Turning off the main Tel-Aviv highway at Ramlah, the road leads via the old town of **Lod (Lydda)**, thought to be the birthplace (and place of burial) of St. George, the Patron-Saint of England. It is also the scene of his slaying the dragon. Israel's **Ben Gurion International Airport** (formerly Lod Airport) is a short distance from this town. The road continues north and enters the Sharon Valley.

THE PLAIN OF SHARON is the most fertile part of the coastal plain of Israel and extends west of the edge of the Samaria highlands. Its fertility was proverbial in Bible times. Its roses, possibly the Narcissus, are mentioned in the Song of Songs (2:1). The Sharon is closely settled today by Israeli farmers, many of whom suffered the manifold hardship inherent in pioneer settlement, notably the scourge of malaria with which the plain was stricken not very long ago.

Megiddo-Armageddon — Excavated hill

Not far from the town of Petach-Tikva (Doorway of hope) to the east are the springs and sources of the Yarkon river and near them are the ruins of the fortress of Antipatris, built by Herod and named for his father, Antipater. St. Paul was brought here, with a Roman escort, on his way to Caesarea (Acts 23 : 31—35).

The road continues north through the green, developed and settled Plain of Sharon, parallel to the Tel Aviv—Haifa coastal highway. At Hadera we turn right (east) and continue past Pardess-Hanna and through the "Eeron-Pass" (Wadi Ara) — an ancient important trade and military route — to the Valley of Jezreel-Esdraelon. Turning left at the "Lajjun" crossroads (straight, to Afula, right, to Jenin and Samaria) we come to the mound and ruins of Megiddo.

MEGIDDO (ARMAGEDDON)— Rev. 16:16) was an important city in north central Israel overlooking the Plain of Jezreel-Esdraelon. Its strategic location gave it a historic importance outweighing its size. The importance of Megiddo was due to its domination of the intersection of two vitally important ancient routes; (a) the natural track running northwest and southeast across the edge of the Plain of Jezreel-Esdraelon and roughly paralleling the Carmel Ridge — a road which at its western end led to the Mediterranean port of Acre (and thence north to the Phoenician cities of Tyre and Sidon), and at its other end branched eastwards towards the Jordan depression and directly southwards to Jerusalem; (b) the most direct of three routes cutting through the Carmel Ridge from the Plain of Sharon in a northeast direction at the narrow Eeron Pass, the most vital route between Egypt and Mesopotamia. Over this latter route moved many of the great conquerors of history, from Thutmose III, who in 1468 B.C. stormed Meggido after a hazardous advance through the pass to General Allenby (later Viscount of Megiddo) in World War 1, some 3,386 years later. Egyptians, Assyrians, Canaanites, Israelites, Persians, Greeks, Romans, Saracens, Crusaders from Europe, Turks and British are some of the peoples who have crossed it in force.

The first city of Megiddo appears to have been established by 3500 B.C. It was captured by Egyptians under Thutmose III; thereafter Canaanites held it as a royal city-state until soon after the defeat of King Heber

Megiddo-Armageddon — the water tunnel

by the forces of Deborah and Barak (Judg. 4) Israel gained Megiddo, at least temporarily. In about 1150 or 1100 B.C. Solomon rebuilt it into an important chariot city (1 Kings 9:15; 10:26—29; II Chron. 1:14—17; 9:   ), the headquarters of his fifth administrative district. The wonders of Solomon's Megiddo were unearthed in Stratum IV of the 20 cities piled on top of each other in the mound. Shishak, King of Egypt who "came up against Jerusalem" (1 Kings 14:25; II Chron. 12:9), and took away the treasures of Temple and palace in the fifth year of Rehoboam, also occupied Megiddo in about 915 B.C. King Ahaziah died at Megiddo in about 842 B.C. (2 Kings 9:27). There King Josiah (about 640—609 B.C.), opposing the advance of the Egyptian Pharaoh-nechoh toward Assyria met his untimely death (2 Kings 23:29; 2 Chron. 35:22). The 20th and last city, built on the 70 feet high

rubble of its predecessors perished in about 450 B.C. (W. F. Albright) (or about 350 B.C. — G. M. Shipton). Excavations and archaeological research has yielded vast knowledge for the scientist and Biblical student. Excavations, conducted by the University of Chicago had splendid results. Instigated by the great Egyptologist, James H. Breasted, supported by Rockefeller funds and directed by Clarence S. Fisher (1925—1927), P.L.O. Guy (1927—1935), and Gordon Loud (1935—1939) The original plan of excavation called for peeling off of each of the 20 successive layers of the cities.

Megiddo — Armagedon, symbolic battlefield where the final contest between forces of good and evil is ultimately to take place (Rev 16:16) is based on the fact that Armageddon or the Plain of Megiddo (Jezreel-Esdraelon) time and again has been the scene of violent conflicts.

Haifa — view of city and port

Statue of Elijah — Carmelite Monastery

FROM MEGIDDO TO HAIFA the road goes along the base of the Carmel ridge. It passes by Kibbutz Mishmar' Ha'emek ("Guard of the Valley") Hazoreah and through Yokne'am. Near the wooded southeast headland of Mt. Carmel the dramatic contest between Elijah and the prophets of Baal was held to determine the true God (I Kings 18:17 — 38). Above is seen the Carmelite Monastery of the "Place of burning". The road now continues along the Kishon river and past the "Hill of Priests" where Elijah caused the prophets of Baal to be slain. Joining the Nazareth road we turn left and via Yagur arrive in Haifa.

HAIFA is the main port of Israel with a population nearing 250,000. The city is built at the foot, on the slopes and heights of Mt. Carmel, whose great wedge thrusts northwest-wards right down to the sea leaving at that point only a narrow beach which widens out on its north. Mt. Carmel is the finest mountain in the country and has been justly extolled by the writers of the Sacred Scriptures, as well as by others — for its beauty and has been used by them as a symbol of desirableness and grace. Unlike the rest of the country, Carmel remains green throughout the year on account of the heavy dew which falls on it. It is naturally clothed with a

"The Bahai Shrine on Mt. Carmel

Haifa is the world center of the **Bahai** faith. The golden dome of the Bahai Shrine on the slope of Mt. Carmel is a landmark of the city. The shrine where the Forerunner of the faith, "El Bab", is buried, is surrrounded by a most beautiful garden. It is open for visits from 9 to 12 a.m. daily. The beauty of Haifa, the "tri-fold" city, terracing up the mountain in a sequence of ochre, green, clear-cut cubes, is captivating. On top of Mt. Carmel stands the Carmelite Monastery of St. Elijah, with its beautiful church built over the cave in which the prophet Elijah is said to have dwelt.

Bahai Shrine — archives and library

rich vegetation and oaks are among the trees that are common. Sanctity has been attached to its heights from the earliest times, having been considered the "Mount of God." Here, in the time of Elijah, was the altar of Baal with his priests and prophets and here Elijah confounded them, when their invocation failed and his own to the Lord brought down fire from heaven (1 Kings 18 also Isaiah 35 : 2 and Song of Solomon 7 : 5).

The view from the top of Mt. Carmel is breath-taking — the city and **its harbour, the bay,** across which is the old city of Acre, the mountains of Galilee, topped by snow-covered Mt. Hermon in the north-east and the Industrial zone around the bay (most beautiful also at night when all the lights are on.).

VISITS IN HAIFA AND ON MT. CARMEL

The Maritime Museum, the Bahai Shrine, Dagon Grain Elevator, Panorama Road (for views of the city and Bay), the Technion — Israel's Institute of Technology, the Haifa University campus on Mt. Carmel (the Druze villages of Ousefiya and Daliat-el-Carmel and the Carmelite Monastery of "Mouhraka", where Elijah had his contest with the prophets of Baal, are not far from Haifa, on the heights of Carmel).

154

Church of Annunciation (interior)

FROM HAIFA TO NAZARETH

Driving south-east from Haifa, the highway follows the eastern base of the Carmel Ridge, passes through Nesher with its main Israel's Cement Works and by Kibbutz Yagur, one of the largest communal settlements in the country, About 2 miles further a road branches off to the right and leads to Megiddo, via Yokne'am (see Megiddo-Haifa road). Crossing a bridge over the Kishon River (Judg. 5:19, 1 Kings 18:40), the road ascends the wooded hillocks which divide the coastal Plain of Zebulun from the great Valley of Jezreel-Esdraelon (on the left is Kibbutz Sha'ar-Ha'amakim — "Gate of the valleys") and arrives at the town of Tiv'on.

BETH-SHE'ARIM, A road branches off the main highway, winding down to the right, and comes to the excavated area of Beth-She'arim ("House of Gates"), which was an important town in the second century A.D. and Seat of the "Sanhedrin" — the Supreme Court — after the destruction of Jerusalem by the Romans. Ruins of the synagogue which dominated the acropolis are near the entrance, capitals and architectural fragments are scattered all around. The southern incline of the town-hill is cut by natural clefts, many of which house the necropolis of Beth-She'arim. There are more catacombs, chiselled into the soft chalk of the rock-faces than the size of the town would lead one to expect, for Beth-She'arim became, before it was destroyed in the 4th century, a favourite resting place for wealthy and pious Jews of the East.

The main road descends into the Jezreel-Esdraelon Valley, leading east past the pioneering settlement of Nahalal — the first "Moshav" in the country, founded in 1921 (a road to the right leads to Afula via G'vat and Ganeigar). Continuing, the road ascends the hills and past the town of Migdal-Ha'emek (on the right) comes to the Balfour Forest, planted by the Jewish National Fund. A magnificent, breath-taking view of the Jezreel-Esdraelon Valley is obtained from the road and the slope of the hill on which hundreds of thousands of trees were planted.

On the way to Nazareth, which is a few minutes drive from here only, the road passes through the Christian-Arab village of 'Yafa' (Japhia — on the edge of Zebulun — Josh. 19:12), in which, traditionally, was the home of Zebedee, father of the two Apostles James and John (Matt. 4:21, 10:2, 26:37) (for Nazareth-Tiberias — see Afula-Nazareth-Cana-Tiberias road).

HAIFA TO ACRE (AKKO)

The main road leading north passes through the industrial zone of Haifa Bay — oil refineries, cement, glass, electronics, chemicals, steel, etc. Via Kiryat-Bialik and Kiryat-Chaim it comes to the old city of Acre (Hebrew-Akko) — the Cana'anite port in Bible times, which was assigned to the Tribe of Asher but proved untakeable (Judg. 1:31).

Acre is one of old cities of the Holyland. It was an important Phoneician port and later became a chariot city of Solomon, for his imported Cillician horses. It changed its name to Ptolemais in the Hellenistic era (mentioned by St. Paul in Acts 21:7) and retained importance as a Roman colony. The town was a Byzantine Bishopric and was taken by the Arabs in 638. Baldwin I, the Crusader, conquered Acre in 1114

155

Old Acre — old port

During the 13th century Acre was the capital of the diminishing Crusader Kingdom of Jerusalem. Its final fall to the Saracens in 1291 brought an end to Western rule in the Holyland. For several hundred years most of old Acre remained in ruins, changing hands between Arabs, Turks, Egyptians and, even Napoleon fought in vain for it in 1799. It was taken with the rest of Palestine by the British in World War I and since Israel's war of independence in 1948, became an Israeli town where Jews and Arabs live together peacefully. A large Turkish fortress was used here by the British as a prison for members of the underground (mentioned in the book Exodus).

TO NAHARIYA AND ROSH-HANIKRA

The road from Acre to the north passes by the picturesque arches of the Turkish aqueduct which once brought water to the city, and by Kibbutz Lohamei-Hageta'ot (the Ghetto Fighters). Here, in the local museum are exhibits of pictures and documents from the ghettos and concentration camps.

The settlement of Shavei-Zion with its beautiful farms and charming holiday resort — "Beth-Hava" is seen on the left, on the shore of the Mediterranean. The main road passes through the town of Nahariya, which is the most popular seaside summer resort of Western Galilee, with many nice hotels and a beautiful bathing beach. Nahariya was established in 1934 by immigrants from Germany on barren sand dunes near the Mediterranean.

Kibbutz Gesher Haziv, a lovely farming settlement with a very nice, most inviting Guest House, is about 3 miles further north. Nearby, across the road, is the "Club Mediterranean" resort at Achziv.

Crossing the Achziv bridge, named "Gesher Haziv" (Bridge of glory) in memory of 14 members of the "Hagana" who were killed here in 1947, the road continues north, ascends the chalk cliff and comes to Rosh-Hanikra on the border of Lebanon. The closed road beyond the military post leads via Tyre and Sidon to Beirut, capital of Lebanon. A nice cafeteria and a gift shop, as well as cable-cars to the interesting grottos hollowed by the waves of the sea, are operated by members of the settlements in the area, which is called "Sulam Zor" ("Tyre's Ladder").

FROM ACRE (AKKO) TO ZEFAT (SAFED)

A main road leads east from Acre (Akko) through the plain ("Lot of") Zebulun. Ascending the hills, it continues past the large Arab village of Majd-el-krum and comes to the newly established town of Karmiel. Here the road enters the territory of the Tribe of Asher and passes through ancient olive groves — Olives of Asher, that once produced the oil reserved for the annointing of kings.

Continuing past the village of Rama (Ha-rama of Naphtali) and by Kibbutz Parod, the winding road ascends the steep hills overlooking Galilee's wildest and most romantic scenery: In the east, the Sea of Galilee in its cradle of mountains; far in the west, the Mediterranean and Carmel, and in the south, Mt. Tabor and Lower Galilee. Almost 3000 feet above sea level the road, skirting the mountains and passing near Meiron with its shrine of Rabbi Shim'on Bar-Yohai, continues and arrives at Zefat (Safed) — the capital of Upper Galilee (see Tiberias-Upper Galilee road).

Caves at Mt. Carmel

THE COASTAL PLAIN — FROM HAIFA TO TEL-AVIV

The main coastal highway leads south from Haifa through a narrow fertile plain along the shore of the Mediterranean, between the sea and the range of Carmel. The gigantic pile of the **'Chateau des Pelerins'** (Castrum Perigrinorum), the Pilgrims Castle of **Atlit** soon dominates the shore (mile 8), a black threatening silhouette between the blue sea and the ochre shore. **Atlit**, the largest Crusader Castle in Israel, was built in the beginning of the 13th century. The lofty ruined walls of this last Crusader stronghold in the Holy Land, which was conquered by the Moslems in 1291, are a landmark for miles around.

Turning left, off the main highway near Atlit, a road leads east and joins with the old 'inland road'. A short distance from here (turning left), a narrow road ascends the heights through 'Wadi Fallah' and leads to 'Ya'arot Ha'carmel' and to **Kibbutz Beit-Oren** ("House of Pine") with its nice mountain Guest House. The woods on Mt. Carmel are full with age-old ruins, of rock-cut foundations, "high places", Canaanite altars and Phoenician quarries. High up on Mt. Carmel's plateau, turning left, the road leads to Haifa past the University. Turning right at the junction, the road leads to the picturesque Druze villages of Ousefiya and Daliat el-Carmel. It continues to the Carmelite Monastery of "Mouhraka" (see Elijah the Prophet — Mt. Carmel), and descends to the main 'Wadi Milkh' road.

EIN HOD artists village is a short distance from the main 'inland road' (see Atlit — above), on the slopes of the Carmel range overlooking the beautiful, well-cultivated plain, the Castle of Atlit and the blue Mediterranean. Its painters, sculptors, potters and wood-carvers have many of their works at the central gallery and exhibition hall in the village's center.

The Carmel Caves: the prehistoric Caves of Wadi Mughara. In the bold cliffs of the valley of this name, which here comes down to the plain from Mt. Carmel, a few miles south of Ein Hod, several large caverns whose dark interiors make them conspicuous from afar attract the attention of the traveller on the 'inland road'; the largest of them is called Mugharet el-Wad. They are the caves of prehistoric habitation which, in 1928 and later, were excavated by the American Prehistoric Society and the British School of Archaeology. These excavations resulted in important discoveries of prehistoric remains, including a great quantity of flint implements in several different levels. The most worthy finds were skeletons of the Palaeolithic Age, one which appears to be similar to that of the "Galilee Man" found in Galilee, west of Ginnosar (Gennesaret).

ZICHRON-YA'ACOV, one of the oldest Jewish settlements in the country, established in 1882, may be reached from both, the main coastal highway or from the 'inland road'. Like Rishon Le-Zion in the south, Zichron-Ya'acov is well known for its

Caesarea — the Roman Aqueduct

wine cellars. The Mausoleum-Tomb of the Baron Edmond (Benjamin) de Rothschild and his wife Adelaide is at nearby "Ramat-Hanadiv" — a beautiful park occupying a height with a magnificent view.

The road continues south, passes near Benyamina and via Or-Akivah soon comes to Caesarea.

CAESAREA was built in about 20 B.C. by Herod the Great as a sea port and capital of Palestine and named in honour of his friend and benefactor Augustus. The site was that of Strato's Tower and before that a Phoenician stronghold. After him it was the residence and seat of the Roman Procurators. The Jews still retained certain prerogatives in the municipal government of the city, which were resented by a majority of Syrian-Greeks. The disputed fran-

chise of Caesarea caused riots which, after repeated Roman intervention culminated in a pogrom in which twenty thousand Jews were killed. This was the immediate cause of the First Great Jewish Revolt. Pontius Pilate occupied the governor's residence here. In the house of Cornelius the centurion at Cae-

Caesarea — the Pontius Pilate inscription

Caesarea — the Roman Theatre

sarea, Peter, preached to a Gentile congregation (Acts 10:34, 44, 48) St. Paul landed at Caesarea several times (Acts 18:22). He was sent to this city for trial by Felix (Acts 23:23—33), was imprisoned there for two years (24:27) and there made his defence before Festus and Agrippa (Acts 25, 26) and from there sailed in chains for Rome (Acts 27:1).

Caesarea was home of the church fathers. Eusebius, the historian of the early Church was born here in about 264 A.D. The city capitulated to the Moslems in the 7th century.

Caesarea — an arched street

Caesarea — ruins near old port

Caesarea — two Roman statues (white and red) of the 2nd — 3rd cent. A.D.

It was a place of importance in Crusader times and finally sacked and destroyed in 1291, since when it remained desolate. The Roman city occupied an area of nearly 400 acres. The whole circumference of the Byzantine walls was excavated and the foundations of some square towers stand out clearly. The Crusaders, unable to repopulate so large an area constructed a small rectangular Fortress-town protecting the port and the stores. The walls, about 1600 feet from south to north and 1000 ft. from east to west still stand today as they were rebuilt by St. Louis in 1251—52. The Roman remains include those of a theatre at the southwest side (this has been fully excavated, repaired and is used during the Israel Festival in summer), a hippodrome off the road in the east and an aque-

duct in the north near the seashore. Close to the theatre is the settlement of Sdot-Yam and east of the town is the Caesarea Golf course — the only one in the country. Nearby is the Caesarea Hotel.

Nathanya — capital of the Sharon Valley

The main coastal highway continues south and comes to the town of Hadera — half-way between Haifa and Tel-Aviv. Hadera, founded by young idealists in 1890 suffered heavily from Malaria. It took its early settlers many years to drain the swamps and reclaim the soil. A road from here goes east and leads via 'Wadi Ara' (Eeron) to Megiddo and the Jezreel-Esdraelon Valley (see Plain of Sharon).

NETANYA (Nathanya), capital of the Sharon Valley about 20 miles north of Tel-Aviv, was established in 1929. From a number of huts on the sand dunes, surrounded by swamps and marshes, Netanya has grown and developed and is today a large, industrious modern town and a most popular sea-side summer resort with many nice hotels.

The main road to Tel-Aviv passes near the **Wingate Institute** for Physical training, named after the British General Charles Orde Wingate, who was a great friend of Israel before the state was established.

Kibbutz Shefayim is a very nice agricultural settlement off the main coastal road in the west, with a nice, well-run Guest House. The town of **Herzliya** is about 10 miles north of Tel-Aviv. It was established in 1924. Its new part, known as **'Herzliya-on-sea'** is a lovely residential area with top-class, well known hotels on the beach. Closeby, a few minutes drive from town is the large **Tel-Aviv Country Club** and Hotel.

Remark: When travelling from Tel-Aviv to Haifa, please read the above description of the Coastal Highway "backwards", i.e.: Tel-Aviv, Herzliya, Shefa'yim, Netanya, Kefar-Vitkin, Hadera, Caesarea. Atlit, (Ein Hod and Beit-Oren), Haifa.

Caesarea — Crusader wall — main entrance

The Valley of Elah where David slew Goliath

And Jesse said unto david his son, Take now for thy brethren an ephah of this parched corn, and these ten loaves, and run to the camp of thy brethren; and carry these ten cheeses unto the captain of their thousand, and look how thy brethren fare, and take their pledge. Now Saul, and they, and all the men of Israel, were in the valley of Elah, fighting with the Philistines.

1 Samuel 17:17-19

FROM JERUSALEM TO ASHKELON

A road branches off the Jerusalem—Tel Aviv highway near Eshtaol and goes west past Zorah-Samson's birthplace (Judg. 13:2-25 and Beth-Shemesh where the Ark of the Covenant rested for some time after its return by the Philistines (I Sam. 6:9). Near Azekah (Josh. 15:35) the road descends and enters the valley of Elah, the scene of the battle between the Philistines and Israelites when Saul was King. The Philistine army was pitched between Succoth and Azekah just before Goliath, who was from Gath and had not far to come, challenged the Israelites: ...And the Philistine said 'I defy the armies of Israel this day; give me a man, that we may fight together... Hither came David, a young Shepherd boy, hearing the defiance of the champion, who not long after fell headlong, vanquished by a stone hurled by the young Israelite: ...And he took his staff in his hand and chose him five smooth stones out of the brook, and he put them in a shepherd's bag...; and his sling was in his hand; and he drew near to the Philistine... And David put his hand in his bag and took thence a stone, and slung it, and the stone sunk into his forehead; and he fell upon his face to the earth...* (I Sam. 17).

The road passes now through the boundary between the hills of Judea and the plain of the 'Shephelah'. It continues via Beit-Guvrin, a famous city of old, with its Greek, Roman, Byzantine and Crusader ruins. Nearby is seen the mound of Mareshah, in the vicinity of Moreshet-Gath, birthplace of the prophet Micah (Micah 1:1). After a few miles drive the large mound of Lachish can be viewed on the left. Biblical Lachish was besieged by Sennacherib (2 Kings 19:8) and together with Azekah was the last fortress to withstand Nebuchadnezzar in the south (Jeremiah 34:7). The famous Lachish Letters discovered in 1937 contain a correspondence between the commanders of these two strongholds during the last days of the Davidic Kingdom.

Passing the large J.N.F. forest of "The Angels" we now enter the rolling broad plain of the "Lachish Region" strewn with innumerable new settlements.

The Lachish Region is now celebrating its twentieth year of existence. The settlement of the region, formerly a barren desert, with no water, no trees, and no roadways, is one of the glorious chapters of Israeli settlement in the land; and to this day it serves as a living and successful example of this

Kibbutz Negbah — statue of the defenders at War Cemetery

form of settlement. The Lachish Region was, and remains, a model for mass settlement methods; for the creation of scores of new settlements by bringing large numbers of immigrants to the region almost overnight — from the ship to the village. With no prior agricultural or social preparation, without a pause for integration of people of vastly different backgrounds, immigrants were brought from North Africa, Persia, Iraq, India, Eastern Europe, and France — and they, together, achieved the miracle of making the wilderness bloom, in accordace with the vision of David Ben Gurion.

Twenty years of unceasing activity changed the settlers and turned them from new immigrants — most of them lacking a minimal knowledge in agriculture and having no techinical or professional training which would enable them to use agricultural or mechanical tools — into owners of modern, large farms, comfortable houses, and greenhouses of the most advanced type in the world; farmers who raise crops for export to the world's consumer centres, and who display the natural and rooted instincts found in the sons of generations of farmers.

In the centre of the Region lies the immigrant town of Kiriat Gat, not far from Tel Gath, one of the cities of the Philistines, and the home of Goliath.

The road crosses the main Tel Aviv—Beer'Sheva highway, passes near Kibbutz Negbah (a lone settlement which was heroically defended

163

Ashkelon — Archaeological excavations
Two statues of the Roman goddess of Victory at the local National Park.

by its settlers during the 1948 War of Independence) — seen on the right—and not far from the oil fields of Heletz — seen on the left — and comes to Ashkelon.

ASHKELON was in Biblical times one of the chief cities of the Philistines (The others were: Gaza, Ashdod, Gath and Ekron). Here Samson lost his strength when Delilah cut his hair (Judg. 16). The ancient city whose innumerable wells watered a rich oasis, stood on the trade and military routes leading from Egypt to Mesopotamia and from Arabia and the east to the Mediterranean.
Herod the Great, who was born in Ashkelon, beautified the city with colonnades and impressive courts. The Crusaders had their city and port here too.

The first large-scale excavation was started here by Garstang and P. Adams in 1920-22. The site of Philistine Ashkelon was cut by trial ditches with important results. Unfortunately, however, these ditches have completely caved-in and the once bared ruins of the Canaanite and Philistine strata are completely covered. Of the Byzantine and Crusader buildings found on the surface and the excavated ruins of the Hellenist and Roman periods, scarce remains have survived.

The old part of Ashkelon, formerly called Migdal-Ashkelon (mentioned in Josh. 15:37 as Migdal Gad) has been inhabited by new immigrants since 1950. The new part, close to the Mediterranean, built by the South African Company, Afridar, is a popular seaside resort and residential area with nice hotels and lovely shopping center.

Kibbutz Yad Mordekhai is 6 miles south of Ashkelon and was, until the Six Day War in 1967, a border sett-

Wooden wheel near old well at National Park

lement near the Egyptian held Gaza Strip. It was named for Mordekhai Annilevitz, a leader of the Warsaw Ghetto uprising. This tiny settlement held the Egyptian army with its tanks and artillery for a week in 1948. Then it was evacuated, abandoned, captured and destroyed.. Recaptured a few months later, it was resettled and rebuilt and is today a flourishing settlement. A visit to the reconstructed battle area of 1948 and the local Museum are most interesting. The road continues south, across the former border and comes to the Arab city of Gaza on the main highway through Sinai to Egypt. This was the route of the Pharaohs, Romans, Saracens, Crusaders and others.

The main road from Ashkelon to Tel Aviv leads north, via the newly built port-town of Ashdod. Ashdod was one of the five cities of the Philistine Plain which were at the height of their importance during the Hebrew Monarchy (1020—587 B.C.) It is mentioned many times in the Bible; its palaces and temples (Josh. 15:46; Amos 3::9; I Sam. 5) indicate a city of importance. The most famous incident involving Israel and the city of Ashdod is concerned with the Ark of God which was carried to Ashdod by Philistines and taken into the Temple of Dagon there, with disastrous results to both Temple and citizens (I Sam. 5). It was finally restored to Israel.

Yad Mordekhai — statue of Mordekhai Annilewitz

Old Jaffa Cultural Center

Jaffa (Joppa-Yafo) is one of the oldest cities in the world. In old Testament times it was a port for Jerusalem through which Hiram, King of Tyre sent his Cedars of Lebanon for the building of the Temple by Solomon. It was from here that Jonah (1:3) embarked for Tarshish and was swallowed by a "great fish". In Biblical times Jaffa called "Japho" was assigned to the Tribe of Dan (Josh. 19:46), but the great Philistine city did not come under Israel's control until David gained the Maritime Plain. St. Peter lived here at the house of Simon the tanner (Acts 9:43). Old Jaffa's Cultural Center with its nice art galleries, gift-shops and places of entertainment is near the old port which ceased being a port a few years ago, replaced now by Ashdod, a new town some 25 miles south of here.

TEL AVIV — JAFFA

Tel Aviv ("Hill of Spring") is the largest city in Israel with a population of about 500,000. It was founded in 1909 on sand dunes north of the old city of Jaffa which was the oldest port in the country, through which the early immigrants arrived. Planned only as a residential quarter, where the inhabitants could recover in the evenings after work in nearby Jaffa, it outgrew the old city. Tel Aviv is the center of cultural activities of Israel; Theatres, Philharmonic Orchestra, Opera and places of entertainment, as well as industry and commerce. Some ot its main streets are: Allenby, Dizengoff, Ben-Yehuda, Hayarkon (where, on this street along the seashore are most of the large tourist hotels), Nachlat-Benyamin, Ibn Gvirol, Herzl and Rothschild Boulevard.

Tel Aviv (officially called Tel Aviv—Yafo, or Jaffa) is surrounded by many suburbs and neighbouring towns: Bat-Yam and Holon in the south, Ramat-Gan and Bnei Brak in the east and Herzliya in the north, all regarded to be within the "greater Tel Aviv" or "Gush Dan" area.

Tel-Aviv — hotels near beach

Old Jaffa-St. Peter's church

Tel-Aviv — Mann Auditorium & Habima Theatre

LOD (Lydda) International Airport, now renamed "Ben-Gurion Airport" is 15 miles east of Tel Aviv, about 32 miles from Jerusalem, 65 miles from Haifa, 60 miles from Beer-Sheva, 30 miles from Nathanya and 90 miles from Tiberias.

The WEIZMANN INSTITUTE of Science is in Rehovot, about 15 miles south of Tel Aviv. It is devoted to research and to teaching in the natural sciences and was founded by Dr. Chaim Weizmann, who was a famous scientist and the first President of the State of Israel. It comprises departments for Applied Mathematics, Electronics, Nuclear Physics, Isotope Research, Experimental Biology, Biophysics, Organic Chemistry, Polimer Research and Microanalysis. Another scientific institute in Rehovot is the Faculty of Agriculture of the Hebrew University, with its Agricultural Research Station.

YAD WEIZMANN, the National Memorial for Dr. Weizmann is near the late President's home and includes his and his wife's (Vera) graves. The Memorial commemorates the late President's lifelong activities in the spheres of national renaissance, science and culture.

Tel-Aviv — City Hall

Tel-Aviv — Carmel market

HEBREW SONGS

1. "Yerushala'im shel zahav, veshel nechoshet veshel or, halo lechol shira'ich ani kinor" ("Jerusalem of gold, of copper and of light, let me be a violin for all your songs").
   (The above is the refrain to the most popular song by Naomi Shemer — "Jerusalem of gold" —The song that took a city... a song of longing and prayer that became a hymn of victory during the Six Day War in 1967).

2. Hevenu Shalom Aleichem ("We brought peace to you").

3. Eretz Zavat Halav Oudevash ("Land of milk and honey").

4. Simi yadech al yadi, Ani shelach ve'at sheli, Hei, Hei, Daliya, Bakramim yefeflyah.
   ("Put your hand on my hand, I am yours and you are mine, Oh, Oh, vine, beautiful in the vineyards").

5. Hava, nagila hava, nagila hava, nagila
   Ve-nis mekha. Hava nera-nena, hava nera-nena, hava, hava, ve-nis-mekha..
   ("Let's be gay and happy..").

6. Hi-neh ma tov u-ma-na-im shevet achim gam ya-had. (Twice). Hi-neh, ma tov, shevet achim gam ya-had (twice).
   ("How good and pleasant, sitting brotherly together").

7. Ush-avtem mayim besa-son mima'yanei hayeshu'a (twice). Mayim (4 times) Ho mayim be-sason.
   ("You shall draw water from the springs of salvation").

FLOWERS OF ISRAEL

Flowers, the glory of Israel's springtime, bloom in greater variety in Israel than almost anywhere else in the world. Israel's hills and valleys are said to contain 400 varieties of wild flowers not found elsewhere, yet the Bible makes few references to specific flowers, but groups them comprehensively as symbols of life's brevity (Isa. 28:1,4; James 1:10;1 Pet. 1:24); or mentions their use as decorative motifs in the Tabernacle and the Temple (Ex. 25:31,37:17; I Kings 7:26,49). The greatest plant list in Scripture is in the Song of Songs (of Solomon), which contains 74 references to v rious plants — not identified satisfactorily, however, by modern botanists.

Among the commonest flowers of Israel is the Anemone (anemone coronaria), which is related to the buttercup, and which grows in all parts of the country in brilliant reds, delicate pinks, purple blue, white and cream. Acres of these grow along the Sea of Galilee after the February and March rains bring them out in a delicate tapestry thrown across the bare brown shoulders of the ancient countryside. The anemone, sharing the deep hues of royal robes, is often identified as the "lily of the field". The "rose of Sharon" has been identified by some as the crocus of the plain; by others, as the yellow or white narcissus or red tulip. Gladioli in Israel belong to the iris family, and are called "sword lilies" because their spiky stem curves like a scimitar. Lilies of many varieties grow in swampy regions like the former Huleh marshes. Roses have always bloomed in Israel, among rocks, in cultivated gardens, in clay pots and on flat-roofed houses. Almond blossom calyxes were models for the cup of the famous seven-branched golden candlestick (Ex. 37:17), just as the calyx of pomegranate flowers suggested ancient crowns. Larkspure, loosestrife, mallows, jasmine, squills, pink flax, and stars of Bethlehem add their colour to the short spring glory.

BIBLICAL REFERENCES — TREES, PLANTS AND FRUIT

Algum trees	— II Chron. 2:8	Juniper (broom)	— 1 Kings 19:4
Almug trees	— I Kings 10:11	Juniper (roots)	— Job 30:4
Aloes (N.T.)	— John 19:39	Lilies	— Song of S. 5:13
Anise (dill)	— Matt. 23:23	Lilies	— Matt. 6:28
Apple (Apricot)	— Song. of S. 2:3	Manna	— Ex. 16:14
Balm (Balsam)	— Jer. 8:22	Melons	— Num. 11:5
Balm (Balsam)	— Ezek. 27:17	Mint	— Matt. 23:23
Barley	— Deut. 8:8	Mulberry	— II Sam. 5:23
Beans	— Ezek. 4:9	Mustard	— Mark 4:31
Bitter herbs	— Num. 9:11	Myrrh	— Prov. 7:17
Box tree	— Isa. 41:19	Myrrh	— Mark 15:23
Briers	— Isa. 55:13	Myrtle	— Zech. 1:8
Burning bush	— Ex. 3:2	Nuts	— Song of S. 6:11
Calamus	— Song of S. 4:14	Oak	— Isa. 44:14
Camphire	— Song. of S. 4:13	Oak	— Gen. 35:8
Cassia	— Ezek. 27:19	Oak	— Zech. 11:2
Cassia	— Ps. 45:8	Olive	— Deut. 28:40
Cedar	— Num. 19:6	Palm	— II Chron. 28:15
Cedar	— Ps. 92:12	Pine	— Isa. 60:13
Chestnut	— Gen. 30:37	Pomegranate	— Song of S. 4:13
Cinnamon	— Song of S. 4:14	Poplar	— Gen. 30:37
Cockle	— Job 31:40	Reed	— Job 40:21
Coriander	— Ex. 16:31	Rose	— Isa. 35:1
Corn (wheat)	— Gen. 41:57	Rose (Sharon)	— Song of S. 2:1
Cucumbers	— Num. 11:5	Shittim (Acacia)	— Ex. 25:10
Cypress	— Isa. 44:14	Spikenard	— Mark 14:3
Desire	— Eccles. 12:5	Sweet cane	— Isa. 43:24
Dove's dung	— II Kings 6:25	Sycamore	— Amos 7:14
Fig tree	— Prov. 27:18	Sycamore	— Luke 19:4
Flax	— Prov. 31:13	Thistles	— Hos. 10:8
Frankincense	— Song. of S. 3:6	Thorns	— Matt. 27:29
Garlick	— Num. 11:5	Tree (Tamarisk)	— I Sam. 22:6
Gourd (Castor)	— Jonah 4:6	Vine	— Judg. 9:12
Green bay tree	— Ps. 37:35	Weeds	— Jonah 2:5
Heath	— Jerm. 17:6	Wheat	— Judg. 6:11
Husks (Carob)	— Luke 15:16	Willow	— Isa. 44:4
Hyssop (reed)	— John 19:29	Willow	— Ps. 137:2
Hyssop	— I Kings 4:33	Wormwood	— Jerm. 23:15

Famous "Jaffa" oranges

OUR VISIT TO ISRAEL

ARRIVED AT . . . . ON . . . .

Staying at . . . . In . . . .

Our guide's name and address . . . .

. . . .

Our driver's name and address . . . .

. . . .

ITINERARY IN ISRAEL

Day & Date	Place	Hour	Programme

Places Visited

Places Visited

INDEX TO PLACE NAMES

אָאִישׁ אֲשֶׁר לֹא הָלַךְ בַּעֲצַת רְשָׁעִים וּבְדֶרֶךְ חַטָּאִים לֹא עָ
עָמָד וּבְמוֹשַׁב לֵצִים לֹא יָשָׁב ׃ כִּי אִם בְּתוֹרַת יהוה חֶפְצוֹ וּבְ
וּבְתוֹרָתוֹ יֶהְגֶּה יוֹמָם וָלָיְלָה ׃ וְהָיָה כְּעֵץ שָׁתוּל עַל פַּלְגֵי מָיִם
אֲשֶׁר פִּרְיוֹ יִתֵּן בְּעִתּוֹ וְעָלֵהוּ לֹא יִבּוֹל וְכֹל אֲשֶׁר יַעֲשֶׂה יַצְ
יַצְלִיחַ ׃ לֹא כֵן הָרְשָׁעִים כִּי אִם כַּמֹּץ אֲשֶׁר תִּדְּפֶנּוּ רוּחַ ׃ עַל

BLESSED is the man that walketh not in the counsel of the ungod=
ly, nor standeth in the way of sinners, nor sitteth in the seat of the
scornful. But his delight is in the law of the LORD; and in his law
doth he meditate day and night. And he shall be like a tree planted by
the rivers of water, that bringeth forth his fruit in his season; his leaf
also shall not wither; and whatsoever he doeth shall prosper. The un=
godly are not so, but are like the chaff which the wind driveth away.

Psalms I : 1=4

King David, Rothschild Manuscript 24, Ferrara (?) Northern Italy ca. 1470, Parchment, pen and ink,
tampera, 16x21 cm. Exhibit at the Israel Museum, Jerusalem.